# The World In My Kitchen

## Sally Brown and Kate Morris

# NOURISH
EAT WELL, LIVE WELL

We would like to thank our families for trying out our experiments, and the following for their help in research, testing and photography: Iona and Asher Butterfield, Megan Clarricoates, Megan Cox, Edward Coxhill, Bryn Crampsie, Davina Ellis, Josiah and Austyn Emmanuel, Freya, Louis and Charlie Ham, Bethan and Carys Jones, Mia Barrow, Charlie Lovell, Olivia and James Martin, Anneli Pope, Serena Haffner, Elliot Tripp, Olive and Belle Walters, Andrew Ward, and Cathy and Alex in Canada. We would also like to thank Liz Beynon, Colin Campsie and Deirdre Taylor.

'Washing Hands' poem by Lily Morris (aged 9, 2003)

Cooking equipment kindly supplied by Lakeland.co.uk

**The World In My Kitchen**
Sally Brown and Kate Morris

First published in the UK and USA in 2016 by
Nourish, an imprint of
Watkins Media Limited
19 Cecil Court
London WC2N 4EZ

enquiries@nourishbooks.com

Publisher: Jo Lal
Managing Editor: Rebecca Woods
Editor: Wendy Hobson
Design/Art Direction: Viki Ottewill
Commissioned Photography: Vanessa Davies
Food Stylist: Rebecca Woods
Prop Stylist: Jessica Georgiades
Production: Uzma Taj

A CIP record for this book is available from the British Library.

ISBN: 978-1-84899-297-9

10 9 8 7 6 5 4 3 2 1

Typeset in Futura and Allatuq
Colour reproduction by XY Digital
Printed in China

**Publisher's Note**
While every care has been taken in compiling the recipes for this book, Watkins Media Limited, or any other persons who have been involved in working on this publication, cannot accept responsibility for any errors or omissions, inadvertent or not, that may be found in the recipes or text, nor for any problems that may arise as a result of preparing one of these recipes. If you are pregnant or breastfeeding or have any special dietary requirements or medical conditions, it is advisable to consult a medical professional before following any of the recipes contained in this book.

**Notes on the Recipes**
Unless otherwise stated:
- Use free-range eggs and poultry
- Use medium-size eggs, fruit and vegetables, unless stated
- Recipes were tested in a preheated fan oven at the °C listed; you may need to adjust temperatures to suit your oven
- Do not mix metric, imperial and US cup measurements
- 1 teaspoon = 5ml  1 tablespoon = 15ml  1 cup = 240ml
- Spoon measures are always level
- Recipe names have been professionally translated; however, regional, spelling and other differences do occur

nourishbooks.com

# Contents

# To the Young Chef

Hold on tight as you are off on an amazing, whistle-stop tour of the globe – and you don't even have to leave home, as the flavours, colours and smells will come to you. Many may be familiar but we'll be putting them together in new and exciting combinations. It's going to be such fun.

Every day, children sit down to their meals – just like you. But they don't all eat the same things. With these special recipes, you have the chance to make and taste some of the wonderful foods other children eat with their families, when they are out and about, and at special celebrations. Children have tried out all these recipes for us – and lots more – so we know you'll be able to follow and enjoy them.

Whatever you are eating, wherever in the world you are, food needs to grow or be reared and lots of people eat mainly what grows near where they live. The plants we grow for food need sunshine, soil and water, but different plants like growing in different temperatures and conditions. So a plant that grows in the hottest parts of the world near the middle, called the Equator, can grow very quickly. But on the top of huge mountains or in the Arctic and the Antarctic, it is so cold that very little can grow. Do you know what kinds of food plants grow where you live?

It is very important that the food we eat contains all the goodness we need to stay healthy. All these recipes don't just taste great, they are good for you, too.

Even if you think you can't cook, you should be able to follow the recipes. And the first thing chefs do before they start cooking, is read the whole recipe, then collect all the things they need – food and pots and pans.

## Sous chef

Since you are a young chef, you may need a little help, perhaps to find equipment or prepare some ingredients, but mostly just to put your delicious dishes in and take them out of the hot oven. Look for the oven-glove icon 🧤 that means you may need a bit of help.

A chef's helper is called a sous chef, so that's what you can call your adult helper. It means they are not as important as the chef! The more often you practise your cooking skills, the less you are likely to need their help.

# To the Adult Sous Chef

**All our recipes have been created especially for your child to cook as independently as possible and they have all been tested and tasted by children so we know they work. Let your child do as much as possible on their own, depending on their age and ability.**

The dishes are based on authentic recipes that we have adapted for children to cook with minimal supervision. We may have reduced the number of ingredients, substituted easy-to-find options or used frozen or canned fruit and vegetables. We have tried to use the same ingredients a number of times so you won't have leftovers in the larder for long.

If your child is not used to some of the spices, try the recipe as printed the first time, then adjust the spice next time. Or add a squirt of lemon juice, as the acid will temper the heat.

Cooking on the hob/stovetop or over an open fire is usual in many places around the world but, for safety, we have adapted most recipes to cook in an oven.

We devised the recipes with healthy eating in mind so most are high in nutrients and low in sugar, salt and fat. Within that healthy balanced diet, you can enjoy a few of our sweet treats.

Most of the recipes are designed to serve two adults and two children. Others can be stored or are for sharing. You'll find this information at the top of the recipe with the preparation and cooking times and oven temperature. Cooking times are based on a preheated fan oven.

Read each recipe through with the child before they start and explain any new techniques (see pages 7–13). Turn on the oven, if necessary, then stand back and let them cook, being there when necessary to get food in and out of the oven, open cans, melt butter or, occasionally, help them use a sharp knife or grater. The oven glove icon 🧤 at the start of a step suggests when the child might need to ask for help.

The recipes were tested in a preheated electric fan oven at the °C temperature listed. Every oven can be different, so adjust temperatures as required and check that the dishes are cooked before serving, especially those containing meat and fish. Food should be piping hot when it comes out of the oven so let it cool a little before your young chef has a try.

# The World In My Kitchen

Have you ever wondered what children in other countries eat? What do they have for breakfast? What does their dinner smell like? How does it taste? Do they sit at the table? Why not recreate some of the colourful, exciting and fun ways children eat around the world?

Some children may sit on the floor, others at a table. Some might buy their breakfast from a hot-food stall in the street outside their home and then munch it on the way to school. Some don't speak while eating, and you might have to eat in silence in many parts of Africa – that could be a bit difficult. And in some other countries, like Venezuela, you are expected to be very chatty!

Why don't you pick some recipes from one of the 14 countries and find out what people wear every day there – are their clothes the same as yours or different? Can you dress the same way? You might turn the heating up to make your house extra warm if you are eating Thai, or open all the windows for chilly Finland!

What does the table look like when they serve the dishes? In China, people eat with chopsticks instead of knives and forks, and sit on large cushions on the floor – can you? People might use both hands to eat, or a knife and fork. The Moroccans use their right hand and serve themselves from big shared dishes in the middle of the table. Think about the country the dishes you are cooking come from. What kind of serving and eating dishes do they use?

Ask an adult to help you look on the internet for information about the country you have chosen. You could also look for local music to play while you are eating.

Wherever you are in the world, you are sure to find that food is an important part of any celebration. Children just like you love the excitement of having a party. There are even parties about food!

In Italy there's an orange festival in a town called Ivrea – can you find it on a map? They throw oranges at each other! The crowds throw tomatoes at La Tomatina festival in Buñol, Spain, and in Delhi, India, there's a mango festival where they have mango-eating and mango-carving competitions, quizzes, and tastings of over 1,100 types of mango. In Russia there is a pancake week, called Maslenitsa, just before Easter, when they celebrate the end of winter and the beginning of spring by eating pancakes – lots of them! They all sound great fun.

# What You Need

You don't need lots of fancy equipment because we want you to get cooking straight away. You'll find most things in your kitchen, and we'll list them on the next few pages. If you need anything else, the recipe will tell you. Remember to get out all your equipment before you start.

## Weighing and measuring

We use spoons, measuring cups and sometimes weigh foods. Just use one set of measurements – don't mix metric, imperial and American cups.

### Measuring in spoons
You need two sizes of spoon: a 5ml teaspoon and a 15ml tablespoon. You will probably find that the ones in your drawer are okay.

### Measuring in cups
We have used a 240ml/8fl oz measuring cup. If you use cup measures, just lightly fill the cup with the ingredients and level the top, don't pack them down. Lots of measuring cups and jugs also have scales or ladders with cup markings on the side.

### Scales
Some kitchen scales would be useful for measuring. Digital scales are more accurate, especially for small quantities.

## Preparing and mixing

### Cutting board or work mat
If you start with a clean cutting board or work mat to work on, it can help you keep your ingredients close to you so you don't spread out too much. It will protect the work surface, too. Swap for a clean one if you are using raw meat or fish. A damp piece of paper towel underneath will stop it from slipping.

### Scissors
Our favourite kitchen tool is a small pair of short-bladed metal scissors. We like using scissors to chop up ingredients from fresh herbs to cherry tomatoes, raw fish to cooked beef (see page 11). The best ones are just like the ones you use for cutting paper, but you should keep a pair specially for cooking.

### Mixing bowl
You will need a mixing bowl that holds between 2 litres/70floz/8 cups and 3 litres/102fl oz/13¼ cups.

We will say 'hello' to you in many different languages as we travel around the world. We will also tell you the English and the original name of each dish.

### Table cutlery and crockery

You'll need a table knife and fork and a large spoon. You'll also need a cup, some plates and shallow bowls.

## Baking

### Baking sheet and baking parchment

We bake lots of recipes on a flat baking sheet. Sometimes we line them with siliconized baking parchment as it is always non-stick. Then any spills go on the paper and do not cook onto the baking sheet. You can also put a casserole dish on a baking sheet to make it safer and easier to move in and out of the oven.

### Pots and pans

Use bowls and pans that are as near as possible to the ones in the recipes. They don't have to be exactly the same but a little bigger is better than a little smaller. If you are making cakes, though, you do need to use the same size as it says in the recipe.

### Oven gloves

Special padded gloves protect your hands and stop the hot oven or pans from hurting when you are using the oven. Always ask your adult helper to move things into or out of the oven, using the oven gloves. 🧤 You won't forget that ovens, pans and cooked food are hot, but do remember that steam is very hot, too. And HOT HURTS.

## Extra equipment

You'll find it useful to have a few more things:

For preparing: **bread knife, can opener, cutters, dredger, lidded freezer container, grater, paper towels, pastry brush, rolling pin, sieve/fine mesh strainer, spatula, strong plastic food bags, wooden spoon.**

For baking: **bamboo kebab sticks, cake pan** and **liners** (18cm/7in size), **cooling rack, foil, freezer container, large ovenproof casserole dish with a lid** (2 litre/70fl oz/8 cup), **loaf pan** and **liners** (450g/1lb), **long-handled heatproof spoon, muffin, shallow bun** and **cupcake pans** and **papers, square roaster** (about 20cm/8in).

# Clean and Tidy

First things first! You need to be safe and clean. If your kitchen worktop is high, you'll find it difficult to reach and might drop or spill things. Use a table instead, where you can stand on the floor instead of wobbling on a stool, and you'll be able to reach everything more easily.

## Getting organized

- Use a clean, damp cloth and detergent to wipe down the surface and make sure your cutting board or work mat is clean too. Ask your adult to use unperfumed sanitizer, especially if you have had raw meat, fish or unwashed vegetables on the surface.

- Tie long hair back out of the way so it doesn't fall into your cooking.

- Now wash your hands with plenty of soap and rinse well. We've got a rhyme to help you remember.

  Washing hands is good to do
  Every time I use the loo,
  Before I cook,
  Before I eat,
  Before I go to bed to sleep.

- Dry them on a clean towel. Always wash your hands again after touching raw meat, chicken or fish, and after breaking eggs.

- Now put on a clean apron. This not only stops your clothes from getting dirty but also stops anything that is on your clothes, like pet hair, getting into the food.

- Wash and pat dry fresh fruit and vegetables before you start to get rid of any dust or earth. Wash your hands afterwards. You may want to peel vegetables like carrots. You may want to ask your adult to help.

## Clearing up

- Don't forget that you need to tidy and wash up when you have finished. Vegetable trimmings can go in the compost, if you have one. Wash up your pots and cutlery, and clean the work surface with a detergent and then sanitizer again.

- Make sure you clean cutting boards thoroughly, especially after you have been cooking with raw meat and fish. Your scissors need to be washed well, too. Ask an adult to help wash them carefully with the blades open so they get really clean.

# How To . . .

Now we are almost ready to start. There are lots of skills to learn but every recipe tells you exactly what to do at every step. On the following pages, we give you a bit more information on techniques that are used time and time again.

## Chop

You will be chopping fresh herbs and tomatoes with scissors. To do this safely, put what you are chopping into a cup or mug, hold the cup handle firmly with one hand, then put the blades of the scissors into the cup and chop away. Your hands are holding the cup or the scissors so there's no chance of snipping yourself.

## Crack

Egg shells are very clever. Their shape makes them very strong, which is why you might find cracking an egg a bit tricky at first. Put a cup or small bowl with a handle on the work surface. Hold the handle tightly with one hand and the egg firmly with the other, then tap the egg in the middle against the edge of the cup a couple of times. Listen. The sound will change when the egg cracks. Now hold the egg over the top of the cup with both hands and push your thumbs into the crack. Pull your thumbs apart slowly so that the egg drops out into the cup or bowl.

If you have food allergies, check the labels if you are using unfamiliar ingredients. Try the recipes with your usual ingredient replacements and you should still be able to enjoy a global experience.

## Fill

When filling loaf pans, cake papers or moving a mixture from the bowl, use this two-spoon method. Take a spoonful of the mixture. Put the loaded spoon low over where you want to drop the mixture and push it off using a second spoon.

## Grate

You may want to ask an adult to help you as graters are very sharp. Hold the grater by the handle and, keeping your fingers away from the grater, rub the block of cheese, the carrot or the fruit down the blades.

## Grease

To stop food sticking to baking pans, drip a few drops of oil on the pan, then brush it over the surface using a pastry brush or a piece of paper towel.

## Line

Cut a piece of baking parchment to the size of the baking sheet and lay it on top. If you brush a little oil on the sheet first, it will keep the baking parchment in place. Use shaped cake-pan or loaf-pan liners.

Try out new techniques, such as popping a pepper or topping and tailing! Spring onions/scallions are great for adding onion flavour without having to use a sharp knife to cut the onion first.

## Measure

To measure liquids, if you have a jar, get the spoon really full by tipping the container and sliding the spoon fully in. It is easy to fill a spoon from a squeezy bottle. We measure over a plate or bowl to catch any drips. To measure dry ingredients, scoop the ingredients into the spoon, then gently pat the top flat with the palm of your hand.

## Mix

Using a fork, whisk or wooden spoon, stir and mix the ingredients together so they are all muddled up.

## Pop

Put a whole pepper on a cutting board with the stalk facing up. Place your thumbs on the top of the stalk, then push them down firmly to 'pop' the pepper. Tear it open with your thumbs and use your fingers to remove the seeds. Now tear it up or use scissors to cut it into pieces.

## Top and tail

Clean the spring onion/scallion in cold water, then trim off the roots at the white end (the tail), using scissors. Trim off the very dark leaves at the other end (the top). Now cut the rest of the onion into small rings – keep the point of the scissors low to the surface of your cutting board and the onion shouldn't spring too much! Put the top and tail in the compost or bin.

# Asia

We are going to look
at the food they eat
in China and Thailand.

Come and meet the Asian elephant with its six toes, or the camel with its two humps, living here.

With long, winding rivers that freeze with the cold in the mountains, and bring refreshing, cool water to the coast, Asia is home to the world's highest mountain covered in snow, Mount Everest.

The huge, sandy Gobi Desert is hot and dry – 'Gobi' means 'place with no water'.

Tangled, hot and steamy jungles are full of curious-looking animals, like the Sunda flying lemur.

The warmer countries of Asia are famous for using fragrant and tasty spices in their food.

**Hello**
**Nín hǎo**
您好

# China

Welcome to the country that invented toilet paper and ice cream! They put milk and rice into the snow to freeze.

Here you can walk on top of the Great Wall of China, which is one of the largest things humans have ever built.

Or you could visit a toy factory as there are more toy factories here than any other country on Earth.

China is also famous for its 15-day New Year celebrations, where families feast on foods that they believe will bring them good luck and happiness.

in English: Chow mein

in Mandarin: Chǎomiàn

in Chinese script: 炒面

Noodles represent long life and it is thought unlucky to cut them. Slurping them noisily, is polite! The star anise in the small drawing is the main spice in five-spice powder.

 # Chow Mein

There are 292 languages in China and the official language is Mandarin. It has no alphabet. Children here have to learn over 7,000 characters, like little pictures, before they are 11 years old.

 20 minutes

 30 minutes

 Preheat to 180°C/350°F/Gas 4

Serves: 2 + 2

## To make:

1 **Cut the cooked beef** into wide strips, using scissors, and put into the casserole dish.

2 **Top and tail the spring onions/scallions,** using scissors (see Top and tail, page 13), then cut the white and pale green parts into small rings (see Chop, page 11) and add to the casserole.

3 **Pop the pepper** (see Pop, page 13), then cut it into finger-size pieces, using scissors. Cut out the thick stems of the cabbage leaves and cut the leaves into strips. Add them, too.

4 **Stir the five-spice powder**, crushed garlic, soy sauce and pepper into the water. Pour it into the casserole. Put the fresh noodles on top, then put on the lid.

5 🧤 **Ask your adult to put the casserole in the oven**, using oven gloves. Bake for 20 minutes.

6 🧤 **Stir carefully** with a long-handled spoon, then cook for 10 more minutes until it is piping hot.

**Serve with a green salad – and try eating the squiggly noodles with chopsticks.**

## Ingredients:

- 250g/9oz **sliced roast beef**
- 4 **spring onions/scallions**
- 1 **red pepper**
- 2 **savoy cabbage** leaves
- 1 teaspoon **Chinese five-spice powder**
- 2 teaspoons **ready-crushed wet garlic**
- 3 tablespoons **dark soy sauce**
- 1 pinch of **ground black pepper**
- 240ml/8fl oz/1 cup **water**
- 300g/10½oz **straight-to-wok noodles**

## Extra equipment:

casserole dish with a lid, long-handled spoon

# Chinese Roasted Peppers

Hear the pop of the peppers when you push out the stems to make this colourful and spicy dish. It's so easy, and you can teach your friends and family how to do it, too! Try serving the peppers hot or cold.

 20 minutes

 40 minutes

 Preheat to 180°C/350°F/Gas 4

Serves: 2 + 2

## Ingredients:

- 4 **peppers** of any colour
- 1 teaspoon **ready-grated wet ginger**
- 1 teaspoon **ready-crushed wet garlic**
- 2 tablespoons **water**
- 1 tablespoon **soy sauce**
- ½ teaspoon **clear honey**
- 1 pinch of **dried chilli/hot pepper flakes**
- 1 teaspoon **sesame seeds**

## Extra equipment:

square roaster ovenproof dish with a lid, long-handled spoon

## To make:

1 **Pop the peppers** (see Pop, page 13), then cut them into finger-size pieces, using scissors. Put them in the ovenproof dish.

2 **Add the grated ginger**, crushed garlic, water, soy sauce, honey and chilli/hot pepper flakes and stir well with a spoon. Put the lid tightly on the dish.

3 **Ask your adult to put the dish in the oven**, using oven gloves. Bake for 40 minutes until the peppers are soft, then stir carefully with a long-handled spoon.

4 Sprinkle with the sesame seeds, then serve.

**Serve the peppers with a mixture of white and brown steamed rice.**

Tiny sesame seeds are black, with their shell on, or white, without it. We use them in cooking to add a tasty crunch but they are also good for us. They contain proteins and oils that help our liver and eyes stay healthy.

in English: Roasted sweet peppers

in Mandarin: Kǎo tián jiāo

in Chinese script: 烤甜椒

in English: Walnut cookies

in Mandarin: He tao su

in Chinese script: 核桃酥

Before they start their school week, Chinese children raise the Chinese red and gold flag and sing the national anthem as loudly as they can.

# Walnut Cookies

In China, the walnut is supposed to bring good luck and happiness to the family. If you use dried apricots instead of the walnuts, they are thought to help make you rich!

 20 minutes

 15 minutes

Preheat to
140°C/275°F/Gas 1

Makes: 24

## To make:

1 **Break the egg** into a cup (see Crack, page 11) and beat with a fork. Tip it into a mixing bowl.

2 **Add the softened butter**, the sugar and vanilla extract. Mix everything together with a wooden spoon (see Mix, page 13).

3 **Add 2 tablespoons of the flour** and mix well.

4 **Add the rest of the flour and mix** really well until all the flour has disappeared into the butter mixture.

5 **Take a tablespoon of the mixture** and use another spoon to push it into one of the holes in the shallow bun pans, then spread the mixture evenly over the bottom of the pan (see Fill, page 12). Fill the other holes in the same way. Gently press a walnut into the top of each one.

6 🧤 **Ask your adult to put the bun pans in the oven**, using oven gloves. Bake for 15 minutes until the biscuits are risen and lightly golden. Leave to cool on a rack.

Serve one or two biscuits with some fresh fruit as an after-school snack. Or make a Tray of Togetherness. This is eight dishes filled with walnut cookies and other treats to welcome special guests.

## Ingredients:

- 1 **egg**
- 115g/4oz/½ cup **butter**, softened
- 70g/2½oz/⅓ cup **caster/ superfine sugar**
- ½ teaspoon **vanilla extract**
- 125g/4½oz/1 cup **self-raising flour**
- 24 **walnut halves**

## Extra equipment:

**wooden spoon**, two 12-hole **non-stick shallow bun pans**, **cooling rack**

# 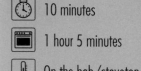 Chinese Tea Eggs

After you have cooked them, peel off the shells of these magical tea eggs to reveal fabulous coloured patterns. Cracking the shells lets the colours in the water make patterns on the egg whites inside the shells.

🕐 10 minutes

🔲 1 hour 5 minutes

🌡 On the hob/stovetop

Makes: 4

## Ingredients:

- 4 **eggs**, at room temperature
- 3 tablespoons **soy sauce**
- 3 **decaffeinated tea bags**
- 1 heaped tablespoon **chopped glacé/candied peel**

## To make:

1 **Put the eggs into the saucepan** and fill with cold water so that the eggs are just under the water.

2 🧤 **Ask your adult to put the pan** on the hob/stovetop over a high heat and bring to the boil. Turn the heat down and boil for 10 minutes. Then ask them to take the pan off the heat and put it into the sink.

3 **Run cold water** into the pan for 5 minutes until the eggs are completely cold.

4 **Gently tap the eggs** with a tablespoon so that the shells crack a little all over. Put the eggs back in the pan and fill it with cold water again. Add the soy sauce, tea bags and glacé/candied peel.

5 🧤 **Ask your adult to boil the eggs** for another 55 minutes. You may need to ask them to top up the pan with more boiling water. Then ask them to take the pan off the heat and put it into the sink.

6 **Run the cold water** into the pan for 5 minutes until the eggs are completely cold. Peel off the shells to see the patterns you have made.

**Eat the patterned eggs as a snack, just as the Chinese do.**

Look out for bird's nest soup, dim sum (dumplings), crispy duck and seaweed on a Chinese menu – all washed down with a cup of Chinese tea.

in English: Chinese tea eggs

in Mandarin: Cháyè dàn

in Chinese script: 茶叶蛋

# Rice

Rice is a staple food, so it is the main part of many people's meal each day. A rice grain is the seed of a plant, and there are over 40,000 types in all colours, shapes and sizes! The outside, or husk, is rubbed off by a machine to give white rice. Basmati, brown and red are the most popular, each with a different flavour and texture. Rice can be cooked in sweet and savoury dishes.

# How to cook long-grain rice

You will need an adult to help you with the saucepan. You might like to serve rice with a few of the meals you make from this book so let's make it really simple. This should be plenty for 4.

1  **Put 1 cup of rice** in a large saucepan and add just under 2 cups of cold water.

2  **Ask your adult to turn on the heat** and boil until the water has almost all disappeared. This will take about 20 minutes.

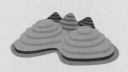

3  **Put the lid on the pan,** switch off the heat and leave it alone for another 15 minutes. You could set the table while you are waiting. Whatever you do, don't peek under the lid yet.

4  **When 15 minutes is up – it's ready!** Where has all the water gone? Give the rice a stir with a fork and you are ready to eat.

## Basmati rice

This is a long, thin grain that grows in the hills of the Himalaya Mountains. It is usually soaked in water before cooking. It tastes slightly nutty and smells amazing. It is a bit like a sponge, mopping up all the spicy flavours of the curry sauces you serve it with.

## Red rice

This long-grain rice has a red-coloured outer layer, so is a wholegrain rice. It has a nutty flavour and cooks quickly. Much of it comes from France or Asia. The red colour from the husk goes into the water when it cooks and colours everything else in the pot red, too.

## Black rice

This is a long-grain, wholegrain rice that is a dark purply-black colour. Many years ago in China, only very important people were allowed to eat it. Because it was so special, the Chinese thought it would make them live longer. They called it 'forbidden rice'.

## Jasmine rice

This is also called 'Thai fragrant rice'. It is a long-grain rice, grown mostly in Thailand. Usually, the husk is rubbed off and the rice is sold as a white rice. It tastes sweet and has a smell a bit like flowers. The grains stick together when they are cooked.

## Italian rice

Italian farmers grow a lot of rice. The most popular are Vialone Nano, Arborio and Carnaroli. They are used to make risotto as the rounder grains go creamy as they cook and soak up all the other flavours. Rice is also used to stuff peppers and thicken soups.

## Brown rice

This type of rice is called wholegrain because you get the whole seed of rice, just as it is when harvested off the plants. The outer layer is called the husk and this is what makes it brown. Brown rice has a sweet, nutty flavour but can take longer to cook than white rice.

# Thailand

Jackfruit and custard apples growing in the Land of Smiles will greet you here among the sun-drenched beaches, exotic wildlife and big cities.

If you meet a crocodile you can stick out your tongue as a crocodile can't!

Menus often include dishes made with chillies and food is often eaten with a fork and spoon.

Stretch your neck to look up at the coconuts growing on the Tree of Life. This is what the Thais call the coconut, as every part of the tree is used for drinking, eating and making things, such as boats, hats, sleeping mats and toothbrushes.

in English: Rice and tofu soup

in Thai: Khaw laea sup taohu

in Thai script: ข้าวและซุปเต้าหู้

Thai people don't shake hands when they meet each other. They press their palms together and bow.

# Rice and Tofu Soup

Slurpy soup with floating rice, this refreshing one-pot meal can be eaten at any time of the day. Thais traditionally eat a savoury breakfast, which is often soup or noodles.

 20 minutes

 30 minutes

 Preheat to 180°C/350°F/Gas 4

Serves: 2 + 2

## To make:

1 **Put the rice in a sieve/fine-mesh strainer** and rinse with cold water. Shake, then put it in the casserole dish. Add the crushed garlic, grated ginger, fish sauce and lime juice.

2 **Add the vegetable stock.**

3 **Top and tail the spring onions/scallions**, using scissors (see Top and tail, page 13), then cut the white parts into small rings and add to the casserole. Stir well. Keep the green parts for later.

4 ✊ **Ask your adult to put the casserole in the oven**, using oven gloves. Cook for 30 minutes until the rice is soft but not mushy.

5 **Chop the coriander/cilantro** in a cup, using scissors (see Chop, page 11), while the soup is cooking. Cut up the dark green parts of the spring onion/scallion.

6 **Dab the tofu dry** with paper towels and cut into cubes, using a table knife.

7 **Stir the soup well.** Spoon the soup into bowls and sprinkle with the coriander/cilantro, spring onion/scallion tops and tofu cubes to serve.

## Ingredients:

- 100g/3½oz/heaped ½ cup **long-grain white rice**
- 1 teaspoon **ready-crushed wet garlic**
- 1 teaspoon **ready-grated wet ginger**
- 1 teaspoon **fish sauce**
- 1 tablespoon **lime juice**
- 1 litre/1¾ pints/4¼ cups **vegetable stock**
- 4 **spring onions/scallions**
- 30g/1oz/½ cup **fresh coriander/ cilantro leaves**
- 300g/10½oz **silken tofu**

## Extra equipment:

**sieve/fine-mesh strainer, casserole dish with a lid, paper towel**

# Thai Chicken Curry

Perfumed and spicy, this curry is made with coconut milk and is full of silky bamboo shoots. Bamboo shoots grow so fast – about 30cm/12in a day. You can almost see them grow in front of your eyes.

 20 minutes

 40 minutes

 Preheat to 180°C/350°F/Gas 4

Serves: 2 + 2

## Ingredients:

- 4 skinless **chicken breast fillets**, about 400g/14oz total weight
- 225g/8oz can of **bamboo shoots**, drained
- 400ml/14fl oz can of **coconut milk**
- 2 teaspoons **Thai green curry paste**
- 1 **red pepper**
- 150g/5½oz **baby sweetcorn**
- 30g/1oz/½ cup **fresh coriander/cilantro leaves**

## Extra equipment:

**can opener, casserole dish with a lid, long-handled heatproof spoon**

## To make:

1 **Cut the chicken pieces into chunks,** using scissors. Try to make the chunks about the same size so they will cook in the same time. Put them into the casserole dish.

2 **Add the bamboo shoots,** coconut milk and curry paste and stir well with a big spoon.

3 **Pop the pepper** (see Pop, page 13), then cut it into chunks, using scissors. Add to the casserole with the sweetcorn and stir again. Put the lid on the casserole.

4 👊 **Ask your adult to put the casserole in the oven,** using oven gloves. Cook for 40 minutes until the chicken pieces are cooked through to the middle (not pink).

5 **Chop the coriander/cilantro** in a cup, using scissors (see Chop, page 11), while the curry is cooking.

6 Sprinkle with the coriander/cilantro to serve.

**Serve on a bed of rice (see page 26) or noodles and eat with a fork and spoon like they do in Thailand.**

The name coconut comes from Portuguese sailors who thought the three small holes on the shell looked like a grinning face, or 'coco'. 'Nut' was added later by the English because it looked like a large nut.

in English: Thai chicken curry

in Thai: Kaeng kai thai

in Thai script: แกงไก่ไทย

in English: Mango salad

in Thai: Yam mamoung

in Thai script: ยำมะม่วง

Peanuts are part of the legume (bean) family and used to be one of the ingredients to make dynamite!

 # Mango Salad

Sweet, salty and spicy, this juicy, crunchy salad is based on the mango and is full of multi-coloured ingredients and plenty of vitamin C. The salad is ideal for a picnic as the lettuce is your edible plate.

 20 minutes

Serves: 2 + 2 as a side dish

## To make:

1 **Pat the mango dry** with some paper towels, then cut it into 1cm/½in chunks, using a table knife. Put it in a serving bowl.

2 **Top and tail the spring onions/scallions**, using scissors (see Top and tail, page 13), then cut the white parts into small rings. Add to the serving bowl.

3 **Chop the coriander/cilantro in a cup**, using scissors (see Chop, page 11). Add to the bowl.

4 **Add the grated ginger**, lemon juice, oil and chilli dipping sauce and mix well with a spoon.

5 **Put the peanuts into a strong plastic food bag** and gently hold the end closed. Smash them with a rolling pin to break them into smaller pieces.

6 **If you are going to eat the salad later**, keep the peanuts in the bag and put the salad in the refrigerator.

7 **When you are ready to eat**, pull the leaves off the lettuce and put them on plates. Spoon the salad into the middle of the leaves and sprinkle with the peanuts.

You can serve the salad on its own or with a chunk of crusty bread.

## Ingredients:

- 425g/15oz can of **mango slices**, drained
- 2 **spring onions/scallions**
- 30g/1oz/½ cup **fresh coriander/ cilantro leaves**
- ½ teaspoon **ready-grated wet ginger**
- 1 tablespoon **lemon juice**
- 1 tablespoon **olive oil**
- 1 teaspoon **sweet chilli dipping sauce**
- 2 tablespoons **blanched peanuts**
- 1 **Little Gem/Bibb lettuce** or similar

## Extra equipment:

**can opener, paper towels, strong plastic food bag, rolling pin**

# Pork Spring Rolls

Roll up, roll up . . . make yourself some of these delicious, crisp little parcels packed with Thai flavours and sprinkled with sesame seeds. They are perfect served hot or cold with a bowl of chilli dipping sauce.

 20 minutes

 20 minutes

 Preheat to 200°C/400°F/Gas 6

Makes: 8

## Ingredients:

- 250g/9oz **low-fat minced/ground pork**
- 1 tablespoon **soy sauce**
- ½ teaspoon **ready-grated wet ginger**
- 1 teaspoon **cornflour/cornstarch**
- 2 **spring onions/scallions**
- 1 **carrot**
- 30g/1oz/½ cup **fresh coriander/ cilantro leaves**
- 8 sheets of **filo/phyllo pastry**
- 2 tablespoons **vegetable oil**
- 1 tablespoon **sesame seeds**

## Extra equipment:

**grater, pastry brush**

## To make:

1 **Put the pork in a mixing bowl** and add the soy sauce, ginger and cornflour/cornstarch. Mix well with a fork.

2 **Top and tail the spring onions/scallions**, using scissors (see Top and tail, page 13). Cut the white parts into small rings and add to the bowl.

3 **Carefully grate the carrot** (see Grate, page 12), then add it to the bowl. Chop the coriander/cilantro in a cup, using scissors (see Chop, page 11). Add it to the bowl and stir everything together well with a spoon.

4 **Divide the mixture into 8 pieces** the same size. Line a baking sheet with baking parchment (see Line, page 12).

5 **Lay out a sheet of pastry** and gently dab it with oil, using the pastry brush. Fold in half along the long side to make a smaller rectangle. Dab with oil again. Now put one of the pieces of pork mix on a bottom corner and roll up diagonally, folding in the extra pastry on each side so you make a small sausage of pastry. Dab the top with oil. Put the parcel on the baking sheet with the join at the bottom. Do the same for the other 7 spring rolls. Sprinkle the tops with sesame seeds.

6  **Ask your adult to put the baking sheet in the oven**, using oven gloves. Bake for 20 minutes until the pastry is crisp and golden and the middle is cooked.

Did you know that carrots were more often purple? Now you can see orange, purple, white, pink and yellow carrots!

in English: Pork spring rolls

in Thai: Poh pei mu

in Thai script: ปอเปี๊ยะหมู

# Africa

We are going to look at the food they eat in Morocco and Mauritius.

Are you a chatterbox like the African Grey Parrot? This parrot can say up to 1,500 words and is the most talkative bird in the world!

Come and meet one, or take a ride on a camel and go inside the ancient pyramids in Egypt.

Clamber on an elephant to the enormous Mount Kilimanjaro or float in a boat on the longest river in the world, the Nile. Beware of the crocodiles!

When you visit Africa, you can choose from sweaty swamps, dry deserts, dripping jungles or the cold, high mountains.

Families in the countryside often grow their own food, which needs a lot of water so they build special ditches to get water to the plants.

Large farms produce coffee, tea and bananas to sell around Africa and the rest of the world.

# Morocco

Even though Morocco is home to the Sahara Desert, very few homes in this hot, dry country have baths. People visit the hammam, a public bath, where they might take three hours to wash and chat — imagine how wrinkly you could get!

Come and visit the noisy souks — Moroccan markets — where narrow passages are filled with strong smells of food and animals, and the dancing snakes will make you smile.

See the vibrant stalls filled with shiny silks, heaps of colourful spices and unusual fruits and vegetables.

Or try a refreshing hot, sweet mint tea while a fortune teller reads your palm and predicts your future.

in English: Harira soup

in Arabic: Shourbet alharira

in Arabic script: شوربة الحريرة

If you are a guest in a Moroccan home, take a gift such as juice or fruit for the adults and yogurt for the children.

# Harira Soup

Get snapping the spaghetti to make this delicious dish, the national soup of Morocco. Full of beans and lots of flavour, this is a meal all in a bowl, flavoured with African spices.

 20 minutes

 1 hour

Preheat to 180°C/350°F/Gas 4

Serves: 2 + 2

## To make:

1 **Put the beans, chickpeas and lentils** in the casserole. Add the lemon juice, crushed garlic, grated ginger and ras el hanout to the water, then pour it over the top.

2 **Chop the tomatoes in a cup**, a few at a time (see Chop, page 11). Snap the spaghetti into short pieces. Add both of these to the dish.

3 **Top and tail the spring onions/scallions**, using scissors (see Top and tail, page 13), then cut the white parts into small rings and put them in the casserole. Stir well and put on the lid.

4 **Ask your adult to put the casserole in the oven**, using oven gloves. Cook for 1 hour until the lentils are soft.

5 **Chop the flat-leaf parsley in a cup**, using scissors (see Chop, page 11).

6 **Stir the casserole** well with a long-handled spoon.

7 **Spoon into bowls** and sprinkle the parsley on top to serve.

You could serve the soup with fresh, warm crusty bread, if you like.

## Ingredients:

- 400g/14oz can of **white beans** such as cannellini, rinsed and drained
- 400g/14oz can of **chickpeas**, rinsed and drained
- 80g/2¾oz/½ cup **green lentils**
- 2 tablespoons **lemon juice**
- 1 teaspoon **ready-crushed wet garlic**
- 1 teaspoon **ready-grated wet ginger**
- 2 teaspoons **ras el hanout spice mix**
- 1 litre/1¾ pints/4¼ cups **water**
- 8 **cherry tomatoes**
- 70g/2½oz **spaghetti**
- 6 **spring onions/scallions**
- 30g/1oz/½ cup **fresh flat-leaf parsley leaves**

## Extra equipment:

can opener, casserole dish with a lid, long-handled heatproof spoon

# Chicken Tagine with Figs

This spicy, sweet stew is traditionally cooked and served in a special pot called a tagine, like the one in the drawing. It is shaped like a witch's hat and often made in bright colours.

 20 minutes

 50 minutes

 Preheat to 160°C/325°F/Gas 3

Serves: 2 + 2

## Ingredients:

- 3 skinless **chicken breast fillets**, about 400g/14oz total weight
- 1 tablespoon **harissa paste**
- 1 teaspoon **ready-crushed wet garlic**
- 1 teaspoon **ready-grated wet ginger**
- ½ teaspoon **ground cumin**
- ¼ teaspoon **ground paprika**
- ¼ teaspoon **ground cinnamon**
- 400g/14oz can of **chopped tomatoes**
- 1 teaspoon **clear honey**
- 4 **spring onions/scallions**
- 6 **semi-dried figs**
- 225g/8oz/1½ cups **couscous**
- 1 tablespoon **olive oil**
- 300ml/10½fl oz/1¼ cups **boiling water** or **stock**
- 30g/1oz/½ cup **fresh flat-leaf parsley leaves**

## Extra equipment:
can opener, casserole dish with a lid

## To make:

1 **Cut the chicken into cubes**, using scissors, and put into the casserole dish. Stir in the harissa paste, crushed garlic, grated ginger, cumin, paprika, cinnamon, tomatoes and honey.

2 **Top and tail the spring onions/scallions**, using scissors (see Top and tail, page 13), then cut the white parts into small rings and add to the casserole.

3 **Cut the figs into 4 pieces each**, using scissors, and add these, too. Stir everything together well with a big spoon, then put the lid on the casserole.

4 🧤 **Ask your adult to put the casserole in the oven**, using oven gloves. Cook for 50 minutes until the chicken is tender and cooked through to the middle (not pink).

5 🧤 **Put the couscous and oil** in a bowl and ask your adult to stir in the boiling water, using a fork. Cover and leave for 5 minutes until the water has disappeared.

6 **Chop the parsley** in a cup, using scissors (see Chop, page 11). Stir the couscous again to fluff up, then stir in the parsley and serve with the tagine.

Serve the dish Moroccan-style, with the tagine piled in the middle of a large plate, surrounded by a ring of couscous and sprinkled with almonds.

When you go into someone's home in Morocco, take off your shoes as a mark of respect, but don't show the bottom of your shoes or your feet as that would be rude.

in English: Chicken tagine with figs

in Arabic:
Tagine aldajaj ma'a alteen

in Arabic script: طاجن الدجاج مع التين

in English:
Cheese and herb pasties

in Arabic:
Fatar'ir aljubna walashab

in Arabic script: فطائر الجبنة والأعشاب

To say, 'No, thank you', when you have had enough to eat, pat your stomach and shake your head.

# Cheese and Herb Pasties

Puff pastry is like a stack of very thin pastry sheets, separated by layers of air. That is why it is so light and crumbly. It is the perfect choice for these cheesy snacks.

  30 minutes

 15 minutes

Preheat to 200°C/400°F/Gas 6

Makes: 8

## To make:

1   **Mix the cheeses and dried oregano** in a mixing bowl. Put the olives and parsley in a cup and chop, using scissors (see Chop, page 11). Add them to the bowl.

2   **Break the egg** into a cup (see Crack, page 11) and beat with a fork. Stir 2 teaspoons of egg into the bowl.

3   **Sprinkle a little flour** on the work surface, using the dredger. Roll out the pastry dough, using a rolling pin, until it is 2.5mm/⅛in thick. Cut it into 8 equal squares with a knife. Put 1 heaped teaspoon of the cheese mixture in the middle of each square of dough.

4   **Mix the water into the egg** in the cup. Using a pastry brush, brush it on 2 sides of the squares, fold the dough into a triangle over the cheese and press the edges together. Pierce the top with the fork. Line a baking sheet with baking parchment (see Line, page 12) and put the parcels on top. Brush with the egg mix and sprinkle with the seeds.

5   👊 **Ask your adult to put the baking sheet in the oven**, using oven gloves. Bake for 15 minutes until puffed, crunchy and golden.

For a Moroccan-style picnic, sit on the floor with your food on a tray in the middle. Help yourself to what is closest, then turn the tray.

## Ingredients:

- 115g/4oz/½ cup **soft cheese**, such as ricotta
- 40g/1½oz/½ cup **grated mild hard cheese**, such as Edam
- 1 teaspoon **dried oregano**
- 6 **stoned/pitted olives**, green or black
- 45g/1½oz/¾ cup **fresh flat-leaf parsley leaves**
- 1 **egg**
- a handful of **plain/all-purpose flour**, for dredging
- 250g/9oz **all-butter puff pastry dough**, at room temperature
- 2 teaspoons **water**
- 2 teaspoons **sesame seeds**

## Extra equipment:

**dredger, rolling pin, pastry brush**

Morocco AFRICA 47

# Lemon, Date and Yogurt Cake

It is easy to make this party cake if you use the yogurt pot as the measure for the other ingredients. Or you can weigh the ingredients as usual, if you like.

 20 minutes

 40 minutes

 Preheat to 160°C/325°F/Gas 3

Makes: 18cm/7in cake

## Ingredients:

- 125g/4½oz pot of **lemon yogurt**
- 2 **eggs**
- 2 tablespoons **Argan** or **vegetable oil**
- 2 tablespoons **milk**
- 2 tablespoons **mixed glacé/candied citrus peel**
- 3 tablespoons **chopped dates**
- 3 yogurt pots of **self-raising flour** (210g/7½oz/1⅔ cups)
- ½ yogurt pot of **caster/superfine sugar** (65g/2¼oz/⅓ cup)

## Extra equipment:

**wooden spoon, 18cm/7in deep cake pan** and **liner, cooling rack**

## To make:

1 **Empty the lemon yogurt** into a mixing bowl, then wash and dry the pot.

2 **Break the eggs** one at a time into a cup (see Crack, page 11) and beat with a fork. Add to the yogurt. Add the oil and milk. Mix with a wooden spoon.

3 **Stir in most of the mixed citrus peel and dates**, but save a handful to decorate the top. (If you have whole dates, you'll need to chop them, using scissors.)

4 **Tip the flour and sugar** into the mixing bowl. Mix all the ingredients together really well until smooth (see Mix, page 13).

5 **Line the cake pan** with the paper liner. Pour the mixture into the pan. Sprinkle the saved chopped fruit on the top.

6 ✋ **Ask your adult to put the cake pan in the oven**, using oven gloves. Cook for 35–40 minutes until the cake is golden and risen and springs back when pressed lightly in the middle. Leave to cool on a rack.

**Enjoy a slice of this delicious cake on its own or with a cup of sweet mint tea. You can also serve it with ice cream as a delicious pudding.**

Argan oil is squeezed from the kernels — the seeds — of the fruit from a tree that looks a bit like an olive but it has a special flavour. It grows very well in Morocco.

in English:
Lemon, date and yogurt cake

in Arabic:
Cake allaimon waltamr walzabady

in Arabic script: كيك الليمون والتمر والزبادي

# Spices and Seeds

Whether crushed seeds or bark, dried fruit, whole leaves, roots or vegetables, spices help our senses explode into action! Long ago people thought spices had special powers to stop you being ill. When they also realized how delicious they were in food, spices became expensive and merchants travelled thousands of kilometres to trade new flavours. Now we enjoy spices from all over the world, not just those from where we live. Many well-known spices, like cinnamon and nutmeg, were first found in Asia. Coriander and poppy seeds came from Europe, chillies and vanilla from the Americas.

## Homemade mixed spice

Try experimenting and make your own mixed spice. Choose 4 of the following spices, add 1 teaspoon of each to a small jam jar with a lid and shake.

- Ground cinnamon • ground nutmeg • ground cloves
- ground ginger • ground caraway seeds

Use it in savoury or sweet recipes by replacing the spices in the recipe with this blend, such as in Chicken Tagine with Figs (see page 44).

# Pepper

Ground pepper, crushed pepper and whole peppercorns are probably the most famous spice. Pepper is a type of plant called a vine that has fruit that looks like berries. Unripe fruits are cooked and dried to make black peppercorns. During Roman times, pepper was so valuable it was as expensive as gold. Today more pepper is used than any other spice. It has a fruity fragrance and is used mostly in savoury dishes. What does it taste like? It can taste strong and sometimes hot and woody.

# Vanilla

Vanilla is the fruit of a plant called an orchid. It grows in hot countries. The long, green beans hang from the plant, looking like the green beans that we eat. The pods are harvested when they are turning yellow, then they are dried and wrapped in blankets. When they are unwrapped and ready to use, they have shrunk and turned black. Inside the pod are thousands of tiny, sticky black seeds. We use the seeds for flavouring ice cream, cakes and cookies. Have you tried our Chinese Walnut Cookies (see page 23)?

# Cinnamon

Also called cassia, cinnamon is the bark of a tree. It is used in whole pieces, called sticks or quills, or ground to a powder. If you smell this dark brown spice it may remind you of Christmas because it is often used in seasonal recipes in Europe and America. Whole quills are also used in many decorations because the fragrance is so welcoming. This spice is well known for being added to sweet recipes, such as cakes and cookies, but can also be used to flavour savoury dishes, such as our Spanish Chicken (see page 100).

# Ginger

Ginger is the root of a plant discovered in China and India thousands of years ago. It has a hot, peppery flavour. Today it can be bought fresh, minced, dried and powdered, pickled and in sweet syrup to use in both sweet and savoury recipes. A warm ginger and honey drink can help a sore throat. To make some, peel about 1cm/½in of root ginger, using the back of a teaspoon to scrape off the skin, then put it in a teapot. Pour over 2 cups of hot water and leave for about 5 minutes. Sweeten it with a little honey, then pour.

# Mauritius

Imagine a tropical island with super-size vegetables and sweet fruits, tall coconut trees, white sandy beaches and clear blue skies – this is Mauritius.

It was created millions of years ago by volcanoes erupting under the Indian Ocean, where there is a jellyfish that lives for ever. The dodo – a huge bird that is now extinct – also lived on Mauritius.

The island has been home to people from lots of different countries so the food they eat is a mixture of Dutch, French, Indian, African and British tastes and flavours.

Roadside stalls sell coconuts with a hole for a straw so you can drink the refreshing coconut water.

in English: Fish salad

in French: Salade de poisson

Dolphins in the waters around Mauritius sleep in pairs, taking it in turns to keep watch for danger.

# Fish Salad

White fish from the sparkling blue seas that surround this island are the perfect idea for this recipe. There's lots of scissor chopping so get ready to snip, snip, snip.

## To make:

1 **Line a baking sheet** with baking parchment (see Line, page 12). Spread the fish out on top and sprinkle with 1 tablespoon of olive oil and a pinch of pepper.

2 👊 **Ask your adult to put the fish in the oven**, using oven gloves. Cook for 10 minutes. It is cooked when the fish will break up into flakes with a fork. Take it out of the oven and put it to one side to cool.

3 **While the fish is cooking**, chop the tomatoes in a cup, a few at a time, using scissors (see Chop, page 11). Watch the juice as it can spray everywhere. Put them into a serving bowl.

4 **Chop the coriander/cilantro in a cup**, using scissors (see Chop, page 11). Add to the serving bowl with the rest of the olive oil and the lemon juice.

5 **Break the cooled fish into small pieces** with your fingers or a fork. Add to the bowl, stir and serve.

**Serve with chunky bread and small sticks of cucumber.**

## Ingredients:

- 4 white **fish fillets**, about 400g/14oz total weight
- 3 tablespoons **olive oil**
- 1 pinch of **ground black pepper**
- 13 **cherry tomatoes**
- 15g/½oz/¼ cup **fresh coriander/cilantro leaves**
- 2 tablespoons **lemon juice**

# Chicken Fingers

Impress your friends with your very own crunchy chicken fingers straight from the oven, covered in golden grains and with some extra tropical flavour.

 20 minutes

 20 minutes

 Preheat to 180°C/350°F/Gas 4

Serves: 2 + 2

## Ingredients:

- 3 skinless **chicken breast fillets**, about 400g/14oz total weight
- 4 tablespoons **plain/all-purpose flour**
- 2 **eggs**
- 1 teaspoon **ready-crushed wet garlic**
- 1 teaspoon **ready-grated wet ginger**
- 1 pinch of **ground black pepper**
- 6 tablespoon **fine polenta/ cornmeal**
- 2 tablespoons **olive oil**

## Extra equipment:

**pastry brush**

## To make:

1 **Cut the chicken breasts up into finger-size pieces,** using scissors. Try to make them all about the same size so they will cook in the same time. Line a baking sheet with baking parchment (see Line, page 12).

2 **Put the flour into a shallow bowl.** Lift the chicken pieces into the bowl and cover all over with flour.

3 **Break the eggs** into a cup (see Crack, page 11) and tip into a second bowl. Add the crushed garlic, grated ginger and black pepper and mix together with a fork. Put the polenta/cornmeal into a third bowl.

4 **Lift a piece of floured chicken** into the beaten egg to cover the flour, and then into the polenta/cornmeal. Put onto the baking sheet. Repeat this with all the chicken pieces. Now wash your hands. Lightly dab the top of the chicken fingers with a little oil, using a pastry brush.

5 🧤 **Ask your adult to put the baking sheet in the oven,** using oven gloves. Bake for 20 minutes until the chicken coating is golden and crunchy, the chicken is tender and the pieces are cooked through to the middle (not pink).

**Serve with our Mango Salad (see page 35).**

Did you know that Mauritius is covered almost entirely (80 per cent) with fields of sugar cane, where the stalks can grow up to 10 metres/30 feet tall?

in English: Chicken fingers

in French: Bâtonnets de poulet

in English: Banana bread

in French: Pain de banane

In Mauritius, sugar is so important it has its own museum, *l'Aventure du Sucre*, to show how it is grown and prepared ready for you to use. Tasting is optional!

# Banana Bread

A bunch is called a hand of bananas and a single one is called a finger. They grow upside-down on large plants, which are part of the herb family.

 20 minutes

 50 minutes

 Preheat to 160°C/325°F/Gas 3

Makes: 450g/1lb loaf

## To make:

1 **Put the cardamom into a strong plastic food bag.** Hold the top loosely and bash with a rolling pin to crush. Sift to separate the seeds from the husk and put the seeds into a mixing bowl. Line the loaf pan.

2 **Peel the bananas** and put into the mixing bowl. Mash well with a fork.

3 **Break the egg** into a cup (see Crack, page 11) and beat with a fork. Add to the mixing bowl.

4 🧤 **Ask your adult to gently warm the oil** in a saucepan. Add the oil and sugar to the mixing bowl and stir, using a wooden spoon.

5 **Put the baking powder**, cinnamon and flour together into the mixing bowl and mix everything together. Pour the mixture into the loaf pan.

6 🧤 **Ask your adult to put the loaf pan in the oven,** using oven gloves. Bake for 50 minutes until risen and golden. Leave to cool on a rack.

Cut into individual slices, then store them in an airtight container. Take them out one at a time for your lunch box, afternoon snack or even a picnic treat.

## Ingredients:

- 3 cardamom pods
- 2 ripe **bananas**
- 1 **egg**
- 5 tablespoons **coconut oil** or **vegetable oil**
- 90g/3oz/½ cup **caster/superfine sugar**
- 1 teaspoon **baking powder**
- ½ teaspoon **ground cinnamon**
- 210g/7½oz/1⅔ cups **plain/ all-purpose flour**

## Extra equipment:

strong plastic food bag, rolling pin, sieve/fine-mesh strainer, wooden spoon, 450g/1lb **loaf pan** and liner, cooling rack

# North America

We are going to look at the food they eat in Canada and Mexico.

Discover the massive mountains and tall trees where the big brown bears live. Gaze across the vast fields of corn. See the winding rivers flow into long lakes. So many things here are super-size – even some of the animals in the sea, like the killer whale.

But there are smaller things, too, like the hummingbird – the only bird that can fly backwards – and the sea otters that hold hands when they are sleeping so they don't drift apart.

This continent is the home of the pumpkin, walnut and blueberry, denim jeans, Bermuda shorts and cowboy hats.

Americans have a national holiday in November called Thanksgiving, at the time when the first European settlers celebrated their successful harvest. Now a national holiday, families get together and eat roast turkey, stuffing, cornbread, mashed potato, gravy and pumpkin pie – that's a huge meal!

# Canada

Magnificent moose, grumbling brown bears and busy beavers can be found living here in the forests of this huge country, where people speak English in some places and French in others.

Look out for the Monarch butterfly using its feet to taste its food.

In winter, the iced lakes are thick enough to drive on. The fishermen drill holes in the ice to go ice fishing. It can be so cold here that they build footpaths underground to help people stay warm.

With so much ice everywhere, ice hockey is the national game.

The sugar maple trees that grow here give us the sweet maple syrup to glug over bacon and pancakes.

in English:
Blueberry pancakes

in French: Crêpes aux bleuets

The Calgary Stampede is a big annual event — a competition and fair for horses, cattle and cowboys and cowgirls. It lasts ten days and they eat over 1,000,000 pancakes!

# Blueberry Pancakes

Deep blue, ocean-coloured blueberries burst through the batter of these pancakes. Pour on maple syrup to make this delicious Canadian weekend breakfast.

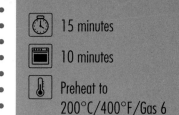

⏱ 15 minutes

▭ 10 minutes

🌡 Preheat to 200°C/400°F/Gas 6

Makes: 6

## To make:

1 **Break the eggs** into a cup (see Crack, page 11) and beat with a fork. Put the eggs, milk and yogurt into a bowl and mix with a spoon (see Mix, page 13).

2 **Put the flour**, baking powder, bicarbonate of soda/ baking soda and sugar into another bowl and mix with a second tablespoon.

3 **Tip the flour into the egg mixture** and mix really well to make a thick batter. Line a baking sheet with baking parchment (see Line, page 12).

4 **Gently stir in the blueberries** with the spoon. Take a heaped tablespoon of the mixture at a time and use another spoon to push it on to the baking sheet to make 6 pancakes.

5 🖐 **Ask your adult to put the baking sheet in the oven**, using oven gloves. Cook for 10 minutes until the pancakes are golden brown, then sprinkle with more fresh blueberries to serve.

**The pancakes are delicious drizzled with maple syrup.**

## Ingredients:

- 2 **eggs**
- 2 tablespoons **milk**
- 2 tablespoons **vanilla yogurt**
- 100g/3½oz/¾ cup **plain/ all-purpose flour**
- ½ teaspoon **baking powder**
- ¼ teaspoon **bicarbonate of soda/ baking soda**
- 2 tablespoons **caster/superfine sugar**
- 40g/1½oz/⅓ cup **blueberries**, plus extra to serve

# Salmon Fishcakes

Bash and mash the potatoes and squish and squash the salmon to make these colourful fishcakes with the pink of the salmon and the green of the herbs.

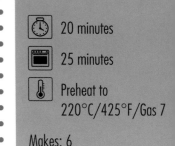

🕐 20 minutes

🔲 25 minutes

🌡 Preheat to 220°C/425°F/Gas 7

Makes: 6

## Ingredients:

- 345g/12oz can of **potatoes**, drained
- 210g/7½oz can of **skinless and boneless salmon**, drained
- 1½ tablespoons **lemon juice**
- 1 pinch of **ground black pepper**
- 30g/1oz/½ cup **fresh dill**
- 1 **egg**
- **vegetable oil**

## Extra equipment:

**can opener, strong plastic food bag, rolling pin**

## To make:

1 **Put the potatoes in a strong plastic food bag** and gently hold the end closed. Smash them with a rolling pin until well mashed, then empty into a mixing bowl.

2 **Use a fork to break up the salmon**, then add it to the bowl. Add the lemon juice and pepper and mix well, using a fork (see Mix, page 13).

3 **Chop the dill in a cup**, using scissors (see Chop, page 11), then add to the fish mixture.

4 **Break the egg** into a cup (see Crack, page 11) and beat with a fork. Add to the fish mixture and mix well.

5 **Line a baking sheet** with baking parchment (see Line, page 12). Shape the mixture into 6 fish cakes all about the same size. Put on the baking sheet and brush the tops with a little more oil.

6 🧤 **Ask your adult to put the baking sheet in the oven**, using oven gloves. Cook for about 25 minutes until piping hot and lightly golden.

**Serve with roasted corn on the cob. Turn on the oven first. Spread a little butter on each corn cob, wrap them in kitchen foil, then put them in the oven at the same time as the fishcakes.**

Did you know that popping corn can be different colours? Look out for purple, green, red, white, black and blue. In some countries, you can buy multi-coloured corn cobs, too!

in English: Salmon fishcakes

in French:
Les croquettes de poisson saumon

in English:
Newfoundland tea buns

in French:
Newfoundland brioches à thé

Put a few grapes in the freezer before you go to school, then they'll be frozen and ready to eat as another type of Canadian after-school snack.

# Newfoundland Tea Buns

A chewy little bun, filled with fruity raisins, children all over Canada often enjoy these buns freshly baked when they arrive home from school needing a tasty snack to keep them going until dinner.

  15 minutes

 10 minutes

Preheat to 200°C/400°F/Gas 6

Makes: 12

## To make:

1  **Mix together the flour**, baking powder and sugar in a mixing bowl with a fork (see Mix, page 13).

2  **Cut the butter into small cubes**, using a table knife. Rub the butter into the flour with your fingertips, a bit like tickling, until it breaks up. The mixture will look like breadcrumbs. Stir in the raisins and lemon juice.

3  **Add 1 tablespoon of the milk and stir**. Everything will start to stick together. Add another tablespoon of milk and stir again until you have a large, soft dough ball. If it doesn't make a dough, add the rest of the milk a little at a time and keep stirring until it does.

4  **Sprinkle a little flour** on the work surface, using a dredger and put the dough on it. Flatten the ball with your hands so that the mixture is about 2cm/¾in thick. Cut out about 12 buns with a 5cm/2in round cutter.

5  **Line a baking sheet** with baking parchment (see Line, page 12). Put the buns on the sheet.

6  👊 **Ask your adult to put the baking sheet in the oven**, using oven gloves. Cook for 10 minutes until slightly risen and golden. Leave to cool on a rack.

In Canada, they serve these buns with dollops of thick cream and jam. You could try them with yogurt instead.

## Ingredients:

- 300g/10½oz/2¼ cups **plain/all-purpose flour**, plus extra for dredging
- 2 teaspoons **baking powder**
- 90g/3oz/½ cup **caster/superfine sugar**
- 100g/3½oz **butter**, softened
- 70g/2½oz/½ cup **raisins**
- 2 tablespoons **lemon juice**
- 6 tablespoons **milk**, at room temperature

## Extra equipment:

**dredger**, 5cm/2in **round cutter**, **cooling rack**

# Fish

Scaly, shiny, small, large, plain, coloured, smooth, rough – fish come in all textures and sizes. They fill the world's oceans, rivers and lakes, and many can be eaten. Fish has lots of special ingredients that help our bodies work well, so we should eat fish each week as it is so good for us. Most fish are caught in the sea. Some are reared in areas called fish farms. There are two types of fish. White fish have delicate white flesh and a little of the good oils that help our bodies stay healthy. Oily fish have darker flesh as they contain lots of the good oils, called omega-3 and omega-6.

# Quick tuna sandwiches

1 **Ask an adult to open a small can of tuna** and drain off the liquid.

2 **Tip the tuna into a bowl**. Add a good squirt of mayonnaise, a pinch of ground black pepper and a squeeze of lemon juice, then mix it all up.

3 **Spread 4 slices of bread** with a little soft butter. Spread the tuna mixture over 2 slices and top with some lettuce, sliced tomato, cucumber slices, a spoonful of sweetcorn kernels or some sliced red peppers.

4 **Pop the other slices of bread** on top and tuck in.

## Tuna

A large, oily fish that lives in warm seas, a tuna fish can be much bigger and heavier than you! (In fact, some types can be as tall as a man.) They can be caught in big nets, but if you buy tuna called skipjack or albacore, the fish is usually caught on a big line, a bit like a fishing rod. That is better than tuna caught in nets as dolphins also swim into the nets and become trapped. You can buy tuna fresh, frozen or in cans. Try out our quick tuna sandwich recipe (below left).

## Salmon

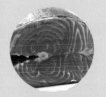

Most fish can only live either in salt water in the sea, or in fresh water in rivers or lakes. Salmon are different and rather special as they hatch in fresh water, then swim out to the salty oceans to grow into adults. When they want to lay their eggs, they have to swim all the way back to the fresh water where they hatched! We eat salmon fresh, frozen and canned. You can also eat smoked salmon, where the fish is 'cooked' in smoke. Have you tried our Salmon Fishcakes (see page 66)?

## Red mullet

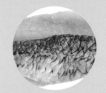

The orange and pink and stripy scales on the red mullet sparkle in the sunshine but before you can eat this member of the white fish family, you need to scrape off those tough scales. Mullet are pinky white inside, too, and have a gentle flavour.

## Sea bass

There are types of sea bass that live in cold seas and also some that live in warm seas around the world. This white fish absorbs other flavours so it is really tasty when cooked with other strongly flavoured ingredients, such as fresh, fragrant herbs or spices.

## Shellfish

Do you like prawns/shrimp? Or crab meat? Have you tried them? These also come from the sea and are from a big group of seafood called shellfish. They can be caught from the wild in the sea, or some types are raised in fish farms. They can be a bit fiddly to eat, but they are delicious.

# Mexico

Imagine trying to learn 68 different languages! That's how many they speak in Mexico.

They laugh when they hear visitors talk about Chilli con Carne because that means 'chilli with some meat', not 'meat with some chilli'. Mexicans may like their food hot but that's silly!

In Mexico, they often wrap meat and juicy sauces in a flour tortilla parcel and eat it with their fingers. This is called a burrito. This can make a delicious, sticky mess.

Apart from lots of chillies, they cook with peanuts, vanilla, beans, cocoa and coconuts. And they use these local ingredients with foods originally from Europe like pork, lamb, beef, wine and cheeses.

in English: Baked eggs in tomato and chilli sauce

in Spanish:
Huevos rancheros

Wrap this delicious mixture up in a flour tortilla parcel to make a burrito version – watch for drips as you eat it!

# Baked Eggs in Tomato and Chilli Sauce

How about this for a spicy weekend brunch to treat friends and family? Download some Mexican music and say, 'Hola!'.

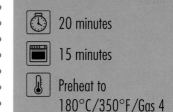

🕐 20 minutes

🔲 15 minutes

🌡 Preheat to 180°C/350°F/Gas 4

Serves: 2 + 2

## To make:

1  **Put the tomatoes in a cup and chop**, using scissors (see Chop, page 11). Add the chilli powder and crushed garlic and stir with a fork. Pour it into an ovenproof dish.

2  **Top and tail the spring onions/scallions**, using scissors (see Top and tail, page 13), then cut off most of the green parts but keep them for later. Cut the white parts into small rings and add to the dish. Add the pepper. Mix all the ingredients in the dish together and spread flat. Press 4 dips into the mixture, using the back of a spoon.

3  **Break 1 egg** into a cup (see Crack, page 11), then pour it into one of the dips. Do the same with the other eggs. Sprinkle the grated cheese over the top.

4  👆 **Ask your adult to put the dish in the oven**, using oven gloves. Cook for 15 minutes until the tomatoes are soft and the egg yolks almost cooked.

5  **Cut the saved green onion tops into rings**, then sprinkle on top.

**In Mexico, this is always served on top of a flour tortilla. You could add some avocado slices, too.**

## Ingredients:

- 450g/1lb/3 cups **cherry tomatoes**
- ½ teaspoon **chilli powder**
- 1 teaspoon **ready-crushed wet garlic**
- 4 **spring onions/scallions**
- 1 pinch of **ground black pepper**
- 4 **eggs**
- 4 tablespoons **grated cheese**

## Extra equipment:

**square roaster ovenproof dish**

# Ham and Cheese Quesadillas

Mexicans love to party. They dress up in colourful costumes and celebrate with street theatre and music, parades and fireworks, and tasty food from market stalls, like these toasted parcels.

 20 minutes

 20 minutes

 Preheat to 180°C/350°F/Gas 4

Serves: 2 + 2

## Ingredients:

- **olive oil**, for brushing foil
- 4 small **flour tortilla bread wraps**
- 8 thin slices of **ham**
- 8 tablespoons **grated mature Cheddar cheese**
- 16 **cherry tomatoes**
- 50g/1¾oz **chorizo sausage**
- 1 pinch of **ground black pepper**

## Extra equipment:

4 **squares of foil** about 40 x 30cm/16 x 12in, **pastry brush**

## To make:

1 **Take 4 large squares of foil** and brush each one lightly with oil, using a pastry brush. Put a tortilla wrap on each.

2 **Share out the ham between the 4 wraps**, then sprinkle the cheese over the top.

3 **Chop the tomatoes in a cup**, a few at a time, using scissors (see Chop, page 11), then put them on top of each wrap. Chop the chorizo with scissors and pop it on top.

4 **Fold the foil over so that the wrap is folded in half.** Crunch up the edges to seal each parcel. Spread the parcels out on the baking sheet.

5 ✋ **Ask your adult to put the baking sheet in the oven**, using oven gloves. Cook for 20 minutes until the middle is piping hot – they can open one foil parcel carefully to check.

**Serve wrapped in a fresh foil parcel, if you like, with a spoonful of sour cream and a glass of milk.**

There is a Mexican scorpion that can survive on one meal a year! I wonder if they get rumbly tummies like us!

in English:
Ham and cheese quesadillas

in Spanish:
Quesadillas de jamón y queso

in English: Cornbread

in Spanish: Pan de maiz

Cornmeal/polenta is made from dried sweetcorn kernels that have been ground up into a golden flour.

# Cornbread

You'll need to use your muscles to mix, mix, mix this gooey golden dough that bakes into a delicious bread. You can serve it as a snack or with salads and other dishes.

⏱ 20 minutes

▢ 20 minutes

🌡 Preheat to 180°C/350°F/Gas 4

Makes: 8 buns

## To make:

1 **Break the egg** into a cup (see Crack, page 11) and beat with a fork. Pour into a mixing bowl. Add the oil, creamed corn, cheese and chilli/hot pepper flakes and mix together, using a fork (see Mix, page 13).

2 **Add the cornmeal/polenta,** flour and baking powder and mix together really well, using a wooden spoon.

3 **Brush a little of the extra oil** into 8 holes of the muffin pan (see Grease, page 12).

4 **Take a spoonful of the mixture** and use another spoon to push it into one of the holes in the muffin pan (see Fill, page 12). Fill 7 more holes evenly in the same way.

5 🧤 **Ask your adult to put the muffin pan in the oven,** using oven gloves. Cook for 20 minutes until risen and golden. Serve warm or leave to cool on a rack and serve cold.

Cornbread is delicious served with a bowl of soup, or with our Baked Eggs in Tomato and Chilli Sauce (see page 75). Try adding some frozen peas or chopped chorizo next time to add extra colours and flavour.

## Ingredients:

- 1 **egg**
- 2 tablespoons **olive oil,** plus extra for greasing
- 6 tablespoon canned **creamed corn**
- 4 tablespoons **grated mature Cheddar cheese**
- 1 large pinch of **dried chilli/hot pepper flakes**
- 4 tablespoons **cornmeal/polenta**
- 4 tablespoons **plain/all-purpose flour**
- 1 teaspoon **baking powder**
- 1 pinch of **ground black pepper**

## Extra equipment:

can opener, wooden spoon, pastry brush, 12-hole **muffin pan,** cooling rack

# Salsa with Home-Baked Tortilla Chips

Mexican children eat *eloté* – cooked corn cobs on sticks – like an ice lolly! Watch out for squirts of juice as you chop the tomatoes!

 30 minutes

 10 minutes

 Preheat to 150°C/300°F/Gas 2

Serves: 2 + 2 as a side dish

## Ingredients:

- 4 x 20cm/8in **plain flour tortillas**
- 2 tablespoons **corn oil**
- ½ teaspoon **paprika**
- 10 **cherry tomatoes**
- ½ teaspoon **ready-crushed wet garlic**
- 1 pinch of **ground black pepper**
- ½ tablespoon **lime juice**
- 1 tablespoon **olive oil**
- ½ teaspoon **chilli sauce**
- 2 **spring onions/scallions**
- 1 ripe **avocado**

## Extra equipment:

**pastry brush, cooling rack**

## To make:

1 **To make the tortilla chips,** cut each circle in half with scissors. Cut each one into 3 triangles. Line a baking sheet with baking parchment (see Line, page 12).

2 **Put the corn oil into a cup** and stir in the paprika. Brush the parchment with the oil, using the pastry brush. Put the tortilla pieces on top, then dab with oil.

3 🧤 **Ask your adult to put the baking sheet in the oven,** using oven gloves. Cook for 10 minutes until crisp and golden. Spread out on a cooling rack.

4 **Chop the tomatoes in a cup,** a few at a time, using scissors (see Chop, page 11). Mix with the garlic, pepper, lime juice, olive oil and chilli sauce in a bowl.

5 **Top and tail the spring onions/scallions,** using scissors (see Top and tail, page 13), then cut the white parts into small rings and add to the bowl. Cover and keep in the refrigerator if not serving straight away.

6 🧤 **Ask your adult to help you cut** round the middle of the avocado. You won't be able to cut it right through as there is a big stone/pit in the middle. Twist the two halves so they come apart, then take out the stone/pit. Scoop the flesh out of the skin with a spoon. Cut the flesh into 1cm/½in cubes and stir into the salsa. Serve with the tortilla chips you have made.

How do you know if an avocado is ripe? Give it a gentle squeeze and if it is soft, it is ready to eat. This pear-shaped fruit was once used like butter by European sailors on their way to New Zealand.

in English:
Salsa with home-baked tortilla chips

in Spanish: Salsa y totopos

# Australasia

We are going to look at the food they eat in Australia, New Zealand and the Pacific Islands.

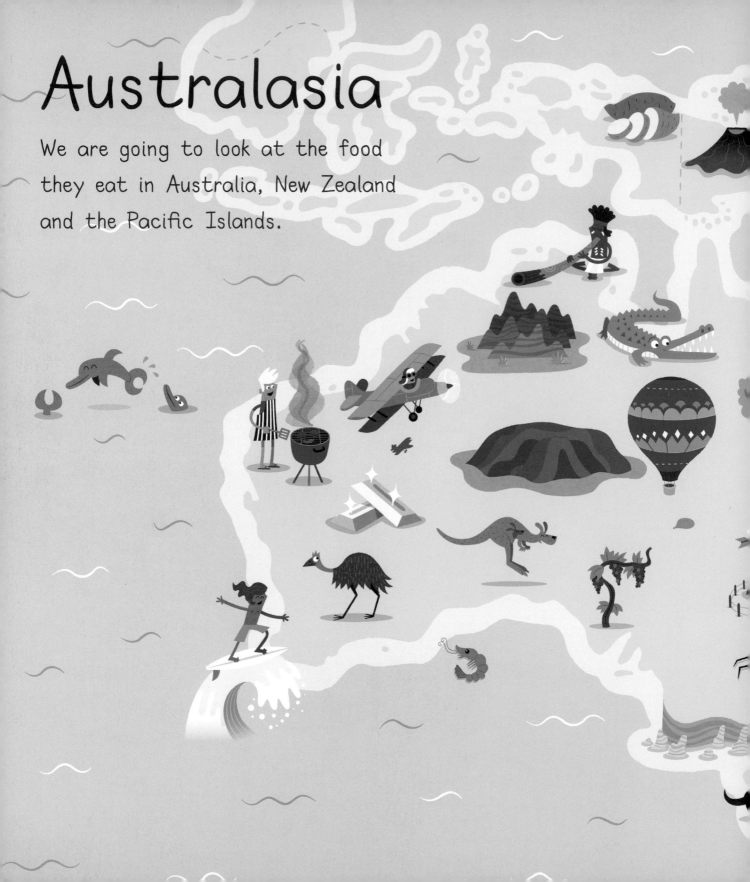

See the sleepy koalas and bouncing wallabies on the vast continent of Australia and the tiny night-time kiwi bird on the mountainous twin islands of New Zealand.

Or try catching one of the curious and colourful fish in the waters around the thousands of remote Pacific islands.

Imagine waking up here in the morning and knowing you are one of the first in the world to see the sun!

Watch out for the heavy coconuts that may fall off the trees, or have fun popping and squeezing the finger limes to discover the delicious citrus-tasting seeds.

# Australia

The world's biggest island is the land of the emu and the kangaroo, which can't walk backwards. Most people live near the coast as the middle is hot desert, called the Outback. Australians love the outdoors and often cook on a barbecue.

# New Zealand

This is one of the newest lands in the world and it has a secret! The two big islands, North and South, are actually one, joined together under the sea. The steep, sunny hillsides are perfect for growing the grapes that become sweet sultanas.

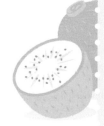

# The Pacific Islands

Swim with turtles that breathe through their bottoms! Or dive through the huge blue waves around these islands, some too small to live on. Yellow bananas and pink-skinned sweet potatoes grow here but there are few shops so food parcels are dropped by parachute.

in English: Baked fish parcels

Australia is home to 20 of the world's most poisonous animals, including the box jellyfish, the eastern brown snake, and the funnel web spider.

# Baked Fish Parcels

This dish gives everyone a present of their own parcel of vegetables and fish. Australia has some of the best seafood in the world – which fish will you choose for your parcels?

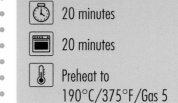

⏱ 20 minutes

▥ 20 minutes

🌡 Preheat to 190°C/375°F/Gas 5

Serves: 2 + 2

## To make:

1  **Lay out the sheets of baking parchment**. Mix the oil, garlic and ginger together in a bowl, then brush over the paper.

2  **Carefully grate the carrot** (see Grate, page 12), then divide it evenly between the 4 pieces and spread it out. Now slice the courgette/zucchini into thin rings, using a table knife, and place evenly on top. Share out the green beans, too.

3  **Put the pieces of fish on top of the vegetables**, one for each parcel.

4  **Top and tail the spring onions/scallions**, using scissors (see Top and tail, page 13), and cut the white parts into small rings. Sprinkle on top of each piece of fish. Add a pinch of pepper, then fold each paper to form a sealed parcel. Put on the baking sheet.

5  🧤 **Ask your adult to put the baking sheet in the oven**, using oven gloves. Cook for 20 minutes until the fish is flaky. Open the parcels carefully.

**Why don't you try adding other ingredients, like tomatoes, to your parcel?**

## Ingredients:

- 2 tablespoons **vegetable oil**
- 2 teaspoons **ready-crushed wet garlic**
- 2 teaspoons **ready-grated wet ginger**
- 2 **carrots**, about 200g/7oz total weight
- 1 **courgette/zucchini**, about 150g/5½oz total weight
- 100g/3½oz frozen **green beans**, defrosted
- 4 pieces of **white fish**, about 400g/14oz total weight
- 4 **spring onions/scallions**
- **ground black pepper**

## Extra equipment:

4 **squares of baking parchment** about 40 x 30cm/16 x 12in, **pastry brush, grater**

# Kiwi Muffins

The symbol of New Zealand, the kiwi is a flightless bird. It's also a large, fuzzy berry. Inside these sweet, pale green muffins you will find its tiny black seeds. They contain an important nutrient called magnesium.

 20 minutes

 25 minutes

Preheat to 200°C/400°F/Gas 6

Makes: 8

## Ingredients:

- 240g/9oz/2 cups **self-raising flour**
- 2 tablespoons **porridge oats**
- 50g/2oz/¼ cup **light soft brown sugar**
- 1 **egg**
- 200g/7oz **kiwi fruit**, about 2 small kiwi fruit
- 120g/4¼oz/heaped ½ cup **plain yogurt**
- 1 tablespoon **lime juice**
- 2 tablespoons **vegetable oil**
- 1½ tablespoons **sunflower seeds**

## Extra equipment:

**wooden spoon**, 12-hole **muffin pan**, 8 **muffin papers**, **cooling rack**

## To make:

1 **Put the flour, oats and sugar** into a bowl and stir with a wooden spoon. This is called the dry bowl.

2 **Break the egg** into a cup (see Crack, page 11) and beat with a fork. Pour into a clean bowl.

3 ✊ **Ask your adult to cut the kiwi fruits in half**. Scoop out the flesh with a teaspoon and add to the egg. If some of the pieces are quite large, use scissors in the bowl to chop the pieces up. Add the yogurt, lime juice and the vegetable oil and stir. This is the wet bowl.

4 **Pour the wet mixture into the dry mixture** and stir until there is no dry mixture to be seen (see Mix, page 13).

5 **Put the muffin papers** in the holes of the muffin pan. Take a spoon of the mixture and use another spoon to push it into one of the muffin papers (see Fill, page 12). Share out the mixture among the muffin papers and sprinkle with the sunflower seeds.

6 ✊ **Ask your adult to put the muffin tray in the oven**, using oven gloves. Cook for 25 minutes until the muffins are risen and golden. Leave to cool on a rack.

**Serve on their own or with vanilla and honeycomb ice cream – called hokey pokey – New Zealand's favourite.**

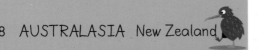

Fresh kiwi fruits can also be eaten by putting one half in an egg cup and eating it with a teaspoon like a hard-boiled egg – a great instant snack!

in English: Kiwi muffins

in English:
Sweet potato and fruit pie

Sweet potatoes, like the ones in the drawing, are not related to potatoes, but are long tubers from a vine called Morning Glory. They have orange flesh and can be used in savoury and sweet recipes.

# Sweet Potato and Fruit Pie

This volcano-shape pie represents the thousands of islands of Oceania, an area in the Pacific Ocean. Most of them were originally volcanos that erupted and broke up larger islands into lots of smaller ones.

 25 minutes

35 minutes

Preheat to 180°C/350°F/Gas 4

Serves 2 + 2

## To make:

1  **Dust the work surface with flour,** using a dredger.

2  **Shape the dough into a ball shape with your hands.** Roll it out once and then turn it and roll and turn until you have a rough circle shape. The dough should be about 20cm/8in across and about 5mm/¼in thick.

3  **Line the baking sheet** with baking parchment (see Line, page 12). Put the dough on the sheet and sprinkle the middle with the polenta/cornmeal, leaving a space all round like an island – this will soak up the juices.

4  **Scoop out the flesh from the potato** and put into a bowl. Use a fork to lightly mash it up. Add the drained pineapple and the spices and stir.

5  **Put the mixture into the middle of the dough.** Keep the space all the way round. Brush the edge with a little of the reserved pineapple juice.

6  **Pinch together the sides of the pie to shape.** You should still be able to see some of the mixture at the top of the pie. It will look a little like a volcano! Brush the pastry with a little of the reserved pineapple juice.

7  ❦ **Ask an adult to put the pie in the oven,** using oven gloves. Cook for 35 minutes until golden.

**Serve on its own or with plain yogurt.**

## Ingredients:

- a handful of **plain/all-purpose flour,** for dredging
- 250g/9oz ready-made **shortcrust pastry dough**
- 3 tablespoons **polenta/cornmeal**
- 240g/9oz/1 cup cooked **sweet potato**
- 240g/9oz/1 cup **crushed pineapple,** drained and juice reserved
- ½ teaspoon **ground cinnamon**
- ¼ teaspoon **ground nutmeg**

## Extra equipment:

**can opener, dredger, rolling pin, pastry brush**

# Fruit

Big, small, beautiful, ugly, smooth and prickly, fruit is one of the largest food families. Fruit contains the seeds that grow into a new plant. Some things we call vegetables are really fruit, like tomatoes and cucumbers. We eat fresh fruit, but it can also be canned, dried, frozen or juiced. Fruit can help us stay healthy as it is full of good things, called vitamins and minerals. Different-coloured fruits look after different parts of your body. Green fights off colds, red keeps heart and joints healthy, purple is good for the brain, orange for eyes and yellow for skin.

# Funny fruit

- The colour orange was named after the fruit. Before that, orange was called red! Orange does not rhyme with any other word in English.

- What is a gorilla's favourite fruit? Ape-ricots!

- What is green and hairy and goes up and down? A gooseberry in a lift!

- What kind of apple has a short temper? A crab apple!

- Why did the banana go to the doctor? Because it wasn't peeling well!

# Fruits with stones

Apricots, plums and avocados all have lots of tasty flesh around a single, large seed in the middle that we call a stone or a pit. This can be planted to grow a new tree. We usually eat the skin of fruits such as the plum because it is soft. But avocado skin is hard, so we sometimes use it like a dish instead and simply scoop out and eat the soft, tasty avocado flesh. Can you think of any other fruit that you can eat like this?

# Fruit from vines

Grapes, cranberries and tomatoes all grow on plants called vines, which climb and spread. They produce fruit from their flowers all along their branches, which are called runners. The fruit can be heavy, so the plants might need to be supported with sticks or they may grow along the ground, like cucumbers or pumpkins. Did you know that you can grow a pumpkin as heavy as an elephant?

# Fruits with lots of seeds

Strawberries, oranges and melons all have lots of seeds. How many seeds do you think there are in a slice of water melon? How many pips in an orange? You can eat the tiny seeds and even some of the bigger ones. Did you know that the strawberry is the only fruit that has its seeds on the outside. Which fruit do you like that has lots of seeds? (An orange has about 6 to 8 pips. The largest number of seeds counted in a water melon is 492!)

# Fast-food fruit

Bananas, peppers and apples are just some of nature's many ready-to-eat fruits, which makes them ideal to eat when you are on the move. Why not try one in your lunch box? Some fruits – like bananas and oranges – have a thick skin that protects the tasty inside. Other fruits we can eat whole – like bell peppers, apples and pears. They may have been transported a long way, so wash them first to clean off the dust.

# Europe

We are going to look
at the food they eat in
Spain, Italy and Finland.

Nod your head and an Albanian will think you have said no. If that isn't difficult, then try speaking the over 200 languages needed to talk to all the people who live in Europe!

Europe is home to the smallest country in the world, Vatican City, and largest, the Russian Federation.

The airport in the city of Brussels in Belgium sells more chocolate than any other place on Earth.

The different weather and crops around Europe mean people have different favourite foods, from delicious hot bacon and egg breakfasts in Britain to delicate sweet pastries and tarts in France and little sandwiches made of ham and cheese in Russia.

And after all that food you might need the loo – Mont Blanc in France has the highest toilets in the Europe at 4,260 metres (nearly 14,000 feet)!

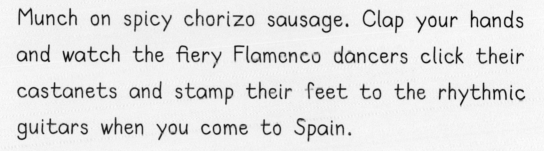

# Spain

Munch on spicy chorizo sausage. Clap your hands and watch the fiery Flamenco dancers click their castanets and stamp their feet to the rhythmic guitars when you come to Spain.

But watch out at Christmas as you will have to wait until 6 January for your presents. And if you are naughty you'll get a lump of black coal instead!

They grow millions of olives here and make almost half of all the olive oil used in the world. Imagine how many trees that needs!

in English:
Baked prawn paella

in Spanish:
Paella de gambas al horno

At New Year in Spain, each person in the family eats one grape on each chime of the clock at midnight to bring good luck for the new year. This tradition is known as The Twelve Grapes of Luck.

# Baked Prawn Paella

This rice dish originates from Valencia. It is cooked in a huge, shallow pan called a paella, which gives the dish its name. National Paella Day is on 27 March in Spain.

 20 minutes

 45 minutes

 Preheat to 180°C/350°F/Gas 4

Serves: 2 + 2

## To make:

1 **Put the water into the casserole dish**, then crumble in the stock/bouillon cube and stir with a large spoon.

2 **Pop the pepper** [see Pop, page 13], then cut it into small pieces, using scissors. Add to the casserole with the rice, paprika, lemon juice and black pepper.

3 **Top and tail the spring onions/scallions**, using scissors (see Top and tail, page 13), then chop the white part into small rings (see Chop, page 11). Add to the casserole with the sweetcorn, tomatoes and prawns/shrimp and stir gently. Put on the lid.

4 🧤 **Ask your adult to put the casserole in the oven**, using oven gloves. Cook for 45 minutes until the rice is soft and the prawns/shrimp are pink.

5 **Chop the parsley in a cup**, using scissors (see Chop, page 11), then sprinkle over the top to serve.

**Serve with wedges of lemon to squeeze over the dish.**

## Ingredients:

- 700ml/24fl oz/3 cups **water**
- 1 **fish stock/bouillon cube**
- 1 **green pepper**
- 185g/6½oz/1 cup **Arborio rice**
- 1 teaspoon **paprika**
- 2 tablespoons **lemon juice**
- 2 pinches of **ground black pepper**
- 4 **spring onions/scallions**
- 100g/3½oz/1 cup canned or frozen **sweetcorn**
- 400g/14oz can of **chopped tomatoes**
- 300g/10½oz/1 cup raw peeled **prawns/shrimp**
- 30g/1oz/½ cup **fresh flat-leaf parsley leaves**

## Extra equipment:

can opener, casserole dish with a lid

# Spanish Chicken

The most precious spice in the world, just a pinch of saffron will colour your dish and give it a honey aroma. The hand-picked stamens from 80,000 saffron crocus plants are dried to produce 2 cups of saffron.

  20 minutes

 30 minutes

Preheat to 200°C/400°F/Gas 6

Serves: 2 + 2

## Ingredients:

- 240ml/8fl oz/1 cup **water**
- 2 pinches of **saffron**
- ½ **vegetable stock/bouillon cube**, crumbled
- 1 pinch of **ground cinnamon**
- 1 pinch of **chilli/hot pepper flakes**
- 2 tablespoons **red wine vinegar**
- 2 tablespoons **clear honey**
- 2 tablespoons **sultanas/ golden raisins**
- 6 **spring onions/scallions**
- 12 **cherry tomatoes**
- 30g/1oz/½ cup **fresh flat-leaf parsley leaves**
- 500g/1lb 2oz skinless **chicken breast fillets**
- 2 tablespoons **toasted pine nuts**

## Extra equipment:

**casserole dish with a lid**

## To make:

1 **Put the water into the casserole dish**. Add the saffron, stock/bouillon cube, cinnamon, chilli/hot pepper flakes, vinegar, honey and sultanas/golden raisins. Stir with a big spoon.

2 **Top and tail the spring onions/scallions**, using scissors (see Top and tail, page 13), then cut into small pieces. Add to the dish and stir.

3 **Chop the tomatoes in a cup**, a few at a time, using scissors (see Chop, page 11), then add to the dish.

4 **Fill the cup with the parsley**, then chop, using scissors as before. Add to the dish.

5 **Cut the pieces of chicken**, using the scissors, into bite-size pieces. Add to the dish, stir everything well and put the lid on.

6 🧤 **Ask your adult to put the casserole in the oven**, using oven gloves. Cook for 30 minutes until the chicken is tender and the chicken pieces are cooked through to the middle (not pink). Sprinkle the paella with the pine nuts to serve.

**Serve the dish with fresh seasonal vegetables, or with a salad and crusty rolls.**

A good meal in Spain is a noisy one with lots of chatting. In fact, if there is a quiet moment someone might say '*Ha pasado un ángel!*' – An angel has just flown over the table!

in English: Spanish chicken

in Spanish: Pollo Español

in English: Fruit tart

in Spanish: Tarta de frutas

Peaches and nectarines are full of a nutrient called vitamin C, which helps us stay healthy.

 # Fruit Tart

Watch the clever puff pastry grow in the oven to make this fruity tart light and crunchy. It would also be fun to make this recipe as little individual tarts instead of one large one.

 15 minutes

 25 minutes

 Preheat to 200°C/400°F/Gas 6

Serves: 2 + 2

## To make:

1 **Line a baking sheet** with baking parchment (see Line, page 12).

2 **Sprinkle a little flour** on the work surface, using a dredger. Roll out the pastry dough, using the rolling pin, to a large rectangle about 1cm/½in thick.

3 **Mark a line round the pastry dough** 1cm/½in from the edges, using a table knife, so it looks like a picture frame. Don't cut all the way through. Put it on the baking sheet.

4 **Sprinkle the ground almonds** over the pastry, staying inside the frame.

5 **Carefully slice the fruit**, using the single blade of the grater (see Grate, page 12). Cover the ground almonds with the fruit slices. Mix together the cinnamon and sugar in a cup, then sprinkle it over the top.

6 **Break the egg** into a cup (see Crack, page 11) and beat with a fork. Use a pastry brush to brush the edges of the pastry with beaten egg.

7 🖐 **Ask your adult to put the baking sheet in the oven**, using oven gloves. Cook for 25 minutes until golden, crisp and puffed up around the outside.

**Serve with yogurt or Mandarin Ice Cream (see page 112).**

## Ingredients:

- a handful of **plain/all-purpose flour**, for dredging
- 200g/7oz **puff pastry dough**, at room temperature
- 2 tablespoons **ground almonds**
- 4 firm **nectarines** or **peaches** or a mixture
- 1 teaspoon **ground cinnamon**
- 1 teaspoon **caster/superfine sugar**
- 1 **egg**

## Extra equipment:

**dredger, rolling pin, grater, pastry brush**

# Italy

Rome is the capital of this boot-shaped country. And in Rome you'll find Vatican City, the world's smallest country and the only one that can lock its gates at night.

Watch out, as Europe's only active volcanos are here. One of them, Vesuvius, erupted over the city of Pompeii nearly 2,000 years ago. Now the city has been dug out of the rubble so you can visit the remains.

If you like pizza and pasta, you'll love Italian food. But which one of the over 300 pasta shapes will you choose? Make fresh pasta in the morning and sit down for a long, lazy lunch before going back to work or school. Do you know how to check if pasta is cooked? They do say that if you throw it at the wall and it sticks, it's ready to eat!

in English:
Two-topping bruschetta

in Italian:
Bruschetta due guarnizone

The tricolour or 3-colour topping has the same colours as the Italian flag: green, white and red. Pizza toppings are often these colours, too.

# Two-Topping Bruschetta

The long coastline of Italy mean fresh fish is available every day. Children in Italy love to make and eat this colourful snack, and it is often enjoyed at school. Why not try inventing your own toppings?

 20 minutes

 8 minutes

 Preheat to 200°C/400°F/Gas 6

Serves: 2 + 2

## To make:

1  **Ask your adult to help you cut** 10–12 bread slices, using the bread knife.

2 **Brush the baking sheet with a little of the oil,** using a pastry brush. Lay the bread flat on the baking sheet and brush the tops with some more oil.

3 **Ask your adult to put the baking sheet in the oven,** using oven gloves. Cook for 8 minutes until crisp and golden. Let them cool before spreading with the toppings.

4 **To make the fish topping,** put the sardines, tomatoes, lemon juice and pepper in a small bowl. Mix with a fork.

5 **Chop the flat-leaf parsley** in a cup, using scissors (see Chop, page 11). Add to the bowl and stir.

6 **Spread the fish topping** on to half the cooled ciabatta bread slices.

7 **To make the tricolour topping,** chop the tomatoes in a cup, a few at a time, using scissors (see Chop, page 11). Put in a bowl.

8 **Tear up the basil leaves** and mozzarella and add to the bowl with a pinch of pepper. Stir with a fork.

9 **Spread the topping** on to the remaining bread slices and serve with the fish bruschetta.

## Ingredients:

- 1 **ciabatta loaf**, about 270g/9½oz
- 1 tablespoon **olive oil**

## Fish topping:

- 135g/4¾oz can of **sardines in olive oil**, drained
- 2 tablespoons canned **chopped tomatoes**
- 1 tablespoon **lemon juice**
- 1 pinch of **ground black pepper**
- 60g/2oz/1 cup **fresh flat-leaf parsley leaves**

## Tricolour topping:

- 12 red or yellow **cherry tomatoes**
- 4 **fresh basil leaves**
- 140g/5oz/1¼ cups **mozzarella**
- 1 pinch of **ground black pepper**

## Extra equipment:

**can opener, bread knife, pastry brush**

# Ricotta and Spinach Lasagne

The Italians often eat outside, called *al fresco*. They use fresh ingredients from local markets and lay the table with flowers and multi-coloured plates and bowls. This is a favourite combination.

20 minutes

30 minutes

Preheat to 180°C/350°F/Gas 4

Serves: 2 + 2

## Ingredients:

- 2 tablespoons **olive oil**, for greasing and to drizzle
- 180ml/6fl oz/¾ cup **passata (Italian sieved tomatoes)**
- 3 sheets of **fresh egg lasagne**, about 115g/4oz total weight
- 6 **fresh basil leaves**
- 400g/14oz can of **borlotti beans**, drained and rinsed
- 110g/4oz/2 cups **spinach leaves**
- 250g/9oz/heaped 1 cup **ricotta cheese**, at room temperature
- 4 tablespoons **milk**
- 1 large pinch of **ground nutmeg**
- 1 large pinch of **ground black pepper**
- 2 tablespoons **grated hard Italian cheese**, such as Parmesan

## Extra equipment:

**can opener, pastry brush, square roaster ovenproof dish**

## To make:

1  **Brush the ovenproof dish with olive oil**, using a pastry brush. Spread a small amount of the passata on the bottom of the dish, using a tablespoon. Lay a sheet of pasta on top. Spread out about half of the remaining passata on top of the pasta.

2  **Tear up 3 of the basil leaves** and scatter them on top of the passata, then make a layer with half the borlotti beans. Spread half of the spinach leaves over the beans, covering the passata.

3  **Squash the ricotta in a bowl**, using the back of a fork. Add the milk, nutmeg and black pepper and whisk. Spread half the ricotta mixture over the spinach layer.

4  **Repeat the layers** with the remaining ingredients: lasagne, passata, basil, beans, spinach, ricotta mixture. For this last layer, cover all the spinach with ricotta or the leaves will dry out. Sprinkle the top with the hard cheese and drip over some more olive oil. Cover with the lid or a large piece of kitchen foil.

5  👆 **Ask your adult to put the ovenproof dish in the oven**, using oven gloves. Cook for 30 minutes until bubbling and steaming hot.

**Serve with a crunchy salad and crusty olive ciabatta.**

Did you know Italians eat pasta with a fork and spoon unless it is lasagne, and then they need a knife?

in English:
Ricotta and spinach lasagne

in Italian:
Lasagne con ricotta e spinaci

in English:
Savoury olive oil crackers

in Italian:
Biscotti all'olio d'oliva

Celery is a plant that is eaten as a vegetable. It originates from Italy and countries nearby. Every part can be eaten.

# Savoury Olive Oil Crackers

Italians love to have very loud conversations at the dinner table. Add these noisy crackers to the menu as they are perfect to serve with soup or salad or on their own as a snack.

 15 minutes

 6 minutes

Preheat to
220°C/425°F/Gas 7

Makes: 6

## To make:

1 **Mix together the flour**, baking powder, celery salt, oil and water in a bowl with a fork, making a smooth, squishy but not sticky dough.

2 **Sprinkle a little flour** on the work surface, using the dredger. Tip out the dough and split it into 4 even-size pieces. Roll each one into a ball.

3 **Flatten and stretch** each of the dough balls by rolling out with a rolling pin until they are thin and like large tongues!

4 **Line a baking sheet** with baking parchment (see Line, page 12). Put the dough shapes on the sheet. Lightly brush with oil and sprinkle with the cumin seeds and Parmesan.

5 **Ask your adult to put the baking sheet in the oven**, using oven gloves. Cook for 6 minutes until the crackers are crisp and golden. Leave on the baking tray to cool completely.

Take them along to your next picnic and serve with the bruschetta toppings (see page 107).

## Ingredients:

- 125g/4½oz/1 cup **plain/ all-purpose flour**, plus extra for dredging
- ½ teaspoon **baking powder**
- 1 pinch of **celery salt**
- 1 tablespoon **olive oil**, plus extra for brushing
- 3 tablespoons **water**
- 1 tablespoon **cumin seeds**
- 1 tablespoon **grated Parmesan cheese**

## Extra equipment:

dredger, rolling pin, pastry brush

# Mandarin Ice Cream

A fruity, creamy mouthful of orange flavour, this is an easy ice cream treat. Cut the mandarins in half and scoop out the segments to make bowls. We'll tell you how to use them in the serving suggestion below.

 20 minutes, plus freezing

Serves: 2 + 2

## Ingredients:

- 225g/8oz/1 cup **mascarpone cheese**, at room temperature
- 170g/6oz/¾ cup **plain yogurt**
- 1 tablespoon **clear honey**
- 8 **mandarin** segments or 3 **orange** segments
- 3 **fresh basil leaves**

## Extra equipment:

**freezer container with a lid**

## To make:

1 **Put the mascarpone** into the freezer container. Using the back of a fork, smash it up with the yogurt and whisk until you have a smooth mixture (see Mix, page 13).

2 **Add the honey** (or you could use orange blossom honey or agave nectar instead) and whisk again.

3 **Cut the mandarin segments into smaller pieces** in a cup, using scissors (see Chop, page 11), then add them to the mix. Tear the basil leaves into pieces and add. Mix in the fruit and leaves with a spoon (see Mix, page 13).

4 **Put on the lid**, then put the container into the freezer for 1 hour.

5 **Stir again**, then put it back into the freezer for another 2 hours or overnight.

Don't just serve the ice cream with extra fruit – anyone can do that! Spoon the ice cream into the scooped out orange skins and pop some fresh basil leaves on the top. Or make them into in ice lollies/popsicles by freezing in moulds or yogurt pots with woooden or plastic sticks, then turn them out when they are frozen.

Ice cream is also out of this world! According to NASA (the North American Space Agency), ice cream is among the top three items most missed by astronauts on space missions.

in English: Mandarin ice cream

in Italian: Gelato di mandarini

# Herbs

Herbs are the leafy part of plants that are often used to flavour our food and to help us feel better. Originally called 'erbs', which is the French name, this is still used in America today. The h was added in the 19th century to make it easier to say in English. Herbs are often green and can grow in a variety of temperatures, whereas spices need hotter climates. They can be easy to grow at home, in the garden or a pot on the windowsill. Many herbs have wonderful aromas. Lemon balm smells like lemon curd and is amazing in fruit salads. Or you could use pineapple sage to make a delicious, sweet, aromatic tea.

# Herb-flavoured butter

**Do you have leftover fresh herbs from some of your recipes?**

1 Chop them all up into really small pieces, using scissors in a cup (see Chop, page 11), then mash them into a piece of softened butter with a little pinch of ground black pepper.

2 Chill the butter, then spread on toast to top with scrambled eggs, or on warm rolls to serve with soup – or just about anything.

## Parsley

Flat-leaf and curly parsley are both popular and will add colour and texture to almost any savoury dish. The flavour is not too strong, so you can still taste the other ingredients. You can buy it fresh, dried or frozen. Have you tried the Cheese and Herb Pasties (see page 47), which are cooked with flat-leaf parsley?

To dry leftover parsley: Tie a bunch of fresh leaves together with string, then hang in a cool, dry place until completely dry. Store in an airtight container.

## Basil

A basil plant has large, deep green leaves and smells amazing, like a perfume. It is the herb most used in pizza, as it tastes fabulous with tomato, mozzarella and olive oil. There are many types, including sweet, Thai, lemon and purple. Keep a pot of basil on the windowsill (the leaves don't like the refrigerator) and add it to your cooking. The seeds are used in a refreshing Indian drink called falooda. We used fresh basil in our Ricotta and Spinach Lasagne (see page 108).

## Mint

Mint flavours the most popular toothpastes. It is quite easy to grow in the garden and will spread unless you keep it in a pot. You use the stem and leaves for a strong flavour and smell. It is used in both savoury and sweet recipes, like roast lamb, fruit salads and even ice cream. There are many kinds of mint – even a chocolate one that smells of chocolate.

Fill a clean sock with a big handful of mint, lavender and chamomile or other scented herbs. Tie up with string and add to your bath for a lovely, scented wash!

## Rosemary

Rosemary grows as a bush with a strong stem, white, pink, purple or blue flowers, and strong-smelling, needle-like leaves. It came from Asia and the Mediterranean but now grows all over the world. It is a popular herb to flavour lamb or bread. Brides used to wear sprigs of rosemary as a symbol of love.

Pull off most of the leaves from a woody stem to make a kebab stick. Thread it with cooked sausage, pepper pieces, cherry tomatoes and button mushrooms. Brush with olive oil, add a pinch of pepper and cook on the barbecue.

# Finland

Huge green forests, thousands of blue lakes and the stunning midnight sun, they say this is where Father Christmas – Joulupukki – lives, who brings presents to children on Christmas Eve.

There is almost no sun in winter, the polar night, but during summer there can be 24 hours of sun. Imagine your day going on for 24 hours.

Massive tall trees cover most of this land, where the largest forests in Europe make playing hide-and-seek especially thrilling. With nearly 200,000 lakes, many of which freeze over in winter, it is no surprise Finns invented ice skates.

The forests are full of berries during the summer and children eat dried berries like sweets.

in English:
Finnish meatloaf

in Finnish:
Lihamureke marjoilla

The Finns eat up to six small meals a day. They have breakfast, then a hot drink with Pulla (see page 123), lunch (often served as early as 11am), afternoon tea, supper and a drink and a snack just before bed.

 # Finnish Meatloaf

⏱ 10 minutes

🍳 50 minutes

🌡 Preheat to 180°C/350°F/Gas 4

Serves: 2 + 2

Cranberries contain a tiny pouch of air and so if you drop one, it is likely to bounce! They grow on vines in bogs and are picked by hand using a special berry scoop.

## To make:

1 **Top and tail the spring onions/scallions**, using scissors (see Top and tail, page 13), then cut them into small pieces and put into a mixing bowl.

2 **Add the meats**, garlic, stock/bouillon cube and pepper. Mix well.

3 **Carefully grate the bread** (see Grate, page 12) to make breadcrumbs. Add them to the bowl.

4 **Break the egg** into a cup (see Crack, page 11) and beat with a fork. Add to the bowl and mix everything up completely – you could use your hands!

5 **Put the liner in the loaf pan**. Spoon the cranberry sauce into the base of the loaf pan and spread it evenly. Add the meat mixture and press down firmly, making sure you push it into the corners.

6 🧤 **Ask your adult to put the loaf pan in the oven**, using oven gloves. Cook for 50 minutes until browned and bubbling at the edges. Ask them to take it out of the oven and cool for 5 minutes, then turn it upside-down on a serving plate so the berries are on top. Cut into 6 slices (2 per adult, 1 per child), using a table knife.

**Serve with mashed potato and Cucumber and Dill Salad (see page 120).**

## Ingredients:

- **3 spring onions/scallions**
- 175g/6oz **minced/ground pork**
- 175g/6oz **minced/ground beef**
- 1 teaspoon **ready-crushed wet garlic**
- 1 **beef stock/bouillon cube,** crumbled
- 1 pinch of **ground black pepper**
- 1 slice of day-old **bread**
- 1 **egg**, beaten
- 2 tablespoons **whole cranberry sauce**

## Extra equipment:

grater, 450g/1lb **loaf pan** and **liner**

# Cucumber and Dill Salad

Dill looks like fine grass and can feel tickly in your mouth. It is good for us and has a great flavour. If you have some left over you can make it into a cup of tea as it is said to be a cure for hiccups!

 10 minutes

Serves: 2 + 2

## Salad ingredients:

- 1 large **cucumber**
- ½ teaspoon **salt**
- 1 tablespoon **caster/superfine sugar**

## Dressing ingredients:

- 30g/1oz/½ cup **fresh dill**
- 120ml/4fl oz/½ cup **white wine vinegar**
- 1 large pinch of **ground black pepper**

## Extra equipment:

**grater, plastic container with a lid**

## To make the salad:

1 **Carefully slice the cucumber thinly**, using the single blade of the grater (see Grate, page 12). Put the cucumber slices into the container.

2 **Sprinkle with the salt** and sugar.

3 **Put the lid firmly** on the container and shake it all about until the cucumber changes and looks transparent or see-through.

## To make the dressing:

1 **Chop the dill in a cup**, using scissors (see Chop, page 11).

2 **Add the vinegar** and pepper and stir.

3 **Pour the dressing over** the cucumber and serve at room temperature.

**Serve with Finnish Meatloaf (see page 119).**

Did you know cucumbers are made up of 95 per cent water? Instead of drinking water you could try munching on cucumbers!

in English:
Cucumber and dill salad

in Finnish:
Kurkkua ja tilli salaatti

in English: Cardamom bread

in Finnish: Pulla

Finland is part of a group of countries known as Scandinavia. When they raise a glass to say 'Cheers!' or 'Kippis', and to toast someone, they always look into the eyes of everyone around the table.

# Cardamom Bread

Bash open the cardamom pods to find the black seeds inside to use in this traditional wheat bread. Pop the loaf into the oven and wait for the sweet, spicy smell to fill the kitchen.

 15 minutes, plus 1½ hours resting

 25 minutes

 Preheat to 200°C/400°F/Gas 6

## To make:

1 **Put the cardamom** in a strong plastic food bag and crush with a rolling pin. Sift out the seeds and put them into a mixing bowl. Add the milk, yeast, salt and sugar.

2 🧤 **Ask your adult to melt the butter**, then leave it to cool.

3 **Add the flour a little at a time**, then add a little melted butter and stir with a wooden spoon. Keep doing this until it is all used up. If the mixture is wet, add some more flour. Press the dough with your finger and if the mixture springs back it has enough flour.

4 **Shape it into a ball**, put in a dish and cover with a clean dish towel. Leave in a warm place for about 1 hour.

5 **Line a baking sheet** with baking parchment (see Line, page 12). Put the dough on the sheet and push and spread it out, using your hands, to make a 20cm/8in circle. Cover again and leave to rise for 30 minutes.

6 **Break the egg** into a cup (see Crack, page 11), then beat with a fork. Brush over the dough.

7 🧤 **Ask your adult to put the baking sheet in the oven**, using oven gloves. Cook for 25 minutes until golden and hollow-sounding when tapped on the base.

**The Finns serve this with milk or coffee. Make buns with the same dough and sprinkle with cinnamon and sugar.**

## Ingredients:

- 8 **cardamom pods**
- 240ml/8fl oz/1 cup **milk**, at room temperature
- 7g/¼oz/2 teaspoons **dried yeast** or 20g/¾oz/½ cake **fresh yeast**
- 1 teaspoon **salt**
- 90g/3oz/½ cup **sugar**
- 500–625g/1lb 2oz–1lb 6¼oz/ 4–5 cups **plain/all-purpose flour**
- 100g/3½oz/½ cup **butter**
- 1 **egg**

## Extra equipment:

**strong plastic food bag, rolling pin, sieve/fine-mesh strainer, wooden spoon, pastry brush**

# South America

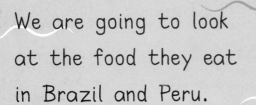

We are going to look
at the food they eat
in Brazil and Peru.

Join the colourful party here, famous for the razzamatazz of the Rio Carnival, the Samba and the Argentine tango.

The Amazon river snakes across the continent, surrounded by the largest tropical rainforest in the world. Even though many of the trees have been cut down, it still covers 5,500,000 square kilometres, that's 2,123,600 square miles.

Many children in remote villages learn to hunt and fish for food instead of shopping for it.

The driest place on Earth is in Chile and the highest spectacular waterfalls are in Venezuela.

Delicious coffee, sweet sugar cane and fragrant cocoa are just some of the foods grown in the hot and sticky north.

Growing in the cooler south are tasty soy beans, lots of potatoes and sweetcorn.

There are huge numbers of cattle, raised for milk but mainly for meat.

# Brazil

Almost half the people in South America live in Brazil and more than three-quarters of them live in its huge cities.

The Brazilians love football so much that they stop everything, including work, to watch an important game.

In South America, there are over 180 languages. You will hear Spanish on TV and see it in newspapers in all countries except Brazil, where they speak a special type of Portuguese.

The food is a mixture of local ingredients and flavours with European and African traditions.

And Brazil really is the home of the Brazil nut!

in English: Cheese puffs

in Portuguese: Pão de queijo

Tapioca flour is made from a root vegetable called cassava or manioc, which you can see in the drawing. It is a plant native to Brazil but now grown in lots of other hot countries.

# Cheese Puffs

20 minutes

10 minutes

Preheat to 180°C/350°F/Gas 4

Makes: 12

These cheese puffs are served all over Brazil – at breakfast, with main meals and as an afternoon snack. You will need adult help for a few steps but it is worth it! Make fresh and eat straight away.

## To make:

1. 👊 **Ask your adult to heat the milk and oil** together in a pan, or in the microwave, until hot but not boiling.

2. **Put the oil and milk into a mixing bowl** and add the flour. Beat with a big spoon until smooth and thick, then let it cool a little.

3. **Break the egg** into a cup (see Crack, page 11) and beat with a fork. Add the egg to the bowl and beat again. Now add the 2 cheeses and mix well.

4. **Dip a pastry brush in a little oil** and brush over the holes in the cupcake pan. Take a spoon of the mixture and use another spoon to push it into one of the holes in the cupcake pan (see Fill, page 12). Fill the other holes in the same way.

5. 👊 **Ask your adult to put the cupcake pan in the oven**, using oven gloves. Cook for 10 minutes or until puffed and risen, just golden and still soft. Leave to cool on a rack.

Serve with fresh avocado and tomato for a savoury snack after school.

## Ingredients:

- 80ml/2½fl oz/⅓ cup **milk**
- 3 tablespoons **olive oil**, plus extra for greasing
- 120g/4¼oz/1 cup **tapioca flour**
- 1 **egg**
- 3 tablespoons **finely grated hard Italian cheese**, such as Parmesan
- 3 tablespoons **grated mature Cheddar cheese**

## Extra equipment:

**pastry brush**, 12-hole **cupcake pan**, **cooling rack**

# Black Bean and Meat Stew

A rich, thick gravy with spicy sausage and beans, this is often made for family gatherings like Sunday lunch and get-togethers.

 20 minutes

 2 hours

 Preheat to 160°C/325°F/Gas 3

Serves: 2 + 2

## Ingredients:

- 3 slices of **streaky bacon**
- 75g/2½oz **chorizo sausage**
- 300g/10½oz **cubed pork**
- 4 **spring onions/scallions**
- 240g/9oz can of **black beans**, rinsed and drained
- 2 teaspoons **ready-crushed wet garlic**
- 480ml/16fl oz/2 cups **water**
- 1 pinch of **ground black pepper**
- 30g/1oz/½ cup **fresh flat-leaf parsley leaves**

## Extra equipment:

**can opener, casserole dish with a lid, long-handled spoon**

## To make:

1 **Cut the bacon into squares,** using scissors. Cut the chorizo into chunks. Put them in the casserole dish and add the cubed pork.

2 **Top and tail the spring onions/scallions,** using scissors (see Top and tail, page 13), then cut the white parts into small rings and add to the dish.

3 **Add the beans,** crushed garlic, water and pepper. Mix well, then put the lid on.

4 ✋ **Ask your adult to put the casserole in the oven,** using oven gloves. Cook for 2 hours, or until the pork is cooked though.

5 **Chop the parsley** in a cup, using scissors (see Chop, page 11).

6 **Stir the casserole** with a long-handled spoon and sprinkle with the parsley to serve.

**This is traditionally served in a big dish with boiled white rice and orange slices.**

If you can't find canned black beans, then use canned kidney beans as the Portuguese do. The name for this casserole comes from the Portuguese for beans: *'feijao'*.

in English:
Black bean and meat stew

in Portuguese:
Feijoada Brasileira

in English:
Pineapple and coconut cakes

in Portuguese:
Bolinhos de abacaxi com côco

Pineapples originally came from Brazil and Paraguay. Did you know that it takes three years for a pineapple fruit to grow enough to be ready to harvest and eat?

# Pineapple and Coconut Cakes

Bring the sunshine into your kitchen by making these sweet and tasty little cakes. They will make a delicious treat when you come home hungry from school, or a special addition to teatime.

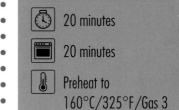

🕐 20 minutes

⬛ 20 minutes

🌡 Preheat to 160°C/325°F/Gas 3

Makes: 8

## To make:

1  **Put the butter**, sugar, coconut and flour in a mixing bowl. Mix with a wooden spoon until light and fluffy (see Mix, page 13).

2  **Put 2 of the pineapple rings in a cup and chop,** using scissors (see Chop, page 11). Add to the mixing bowl.

3  **Break the egg** into a cup (see Crack, page 11), beat with a fork, then add to the bowl. Add 1 tablespoon of the reserved pineapple juice. Mix well with a wooden spoon.

4  **Put the cupcake papers in the holes** of the pan. Take a spoonful of the mixture and use another spoon (see Fill, page 12) to push it into one of the cupcake papers. Share out the remaining mixture.

5  **Cut 1 pineapple ring into 8 chunks.** Gently put a piece on top of each cake. Sprinkle them with the demerara sugar, sharing it out evenly among the cakes.

6  👍 **Ask your adult to put the cupcake pan in the oven,** using oven gloves. Cook for 15–20 minutes until the cakes are risen and golden. Cool on a rack.

**These little cakes are delicious served with coconut yogurt and a glass of milk.**

## Ingredients:

- 50g/1¾oz/3½ tablespoons soft **butter**
- 50g/1¾oz/heaped ¼ cup **caster/superfine sugar**
- 30g/1oz/4 tablespoons **desiccated/dried shredded coconut**
- 75g/2½oz/½ cup **self-raising flour**
- 125g/4½oz canned **pineapple rings**, drained and juice reserved
- 1 **egg**
- 1 tablespoon **demerara sugar**

## Extra equipment:

**can opener, wooden spoon, 12-hole cupcake pan, 8 cupcake papers, cooling rack**

# Cocoa

Just think: what if adventurous people hadn't travelled in their boats far across the sea hundreds of years ago? We might never have tasted chocolate! It comes from a plant that first grew in Mexico and Peru in Central and South America and now grows in Africa and Asia, too. The cocoa tree is very fussy and very delicate. It likes to shelter under bigger trees in the tropical forests so it is protected from the fierce sun and strong winds.

# Quick chocolate milkshake

1 **You will need** a container with a lid that won't leak, like a wide-topped water bottle.

2 **Half fill the bottle** with milk.

3 **Add 2 big scoops** of very soft chocolate ice cream – it is best if you take it out of the freezer about 10 minutes before you start so it is starting to melt.

4 **Fit the lid on tightly**, then shake really hard – jump around the room a bit – until the milk and ice cream are all mixed up.

5 **Pour it into a glass** and drink. Delicious!

## Pod

The cocoa fruit is called a pod and is an oval shape. It comes in colours from bright yellow to a rich red, depending on the type of tree and how ripe the fruit is. The pods look strange on the tree because they grow out of the stem and the main branches. The fruits grow from lots of tiny, delicate flowers that appear on the tree all year round but only a few produce fruit at a time. The pods take five or six months to ripen and be ready to havest. They are cut open to find the cocoa beans, which are the seeds of the plant.

## Powder

We can buy cocoa in a powder to make cakes, ice creams and drinks – have you tried making our Peruvian Chocolate Cakes (see page 143)? Cocoa is not naturally sweet. Cocoa originally grew only in South America and Mexico, where it was known as 'xocolatl', which means warm or bitter liquid. When the Spanish travellers discovered South America in the 16th century and found this amazing plant, they thought the locals said 'chocolate', and the name stuck.

## Seeds

Inside the cocoa pod is juicy, sweet pulp, a bit like marshmallow, which protects the seeds – sometimes as many as 60. Rainforest creatures, like birds and monkeys, enjoy the sweet pulp but spit out the seeds. The farmers hand-cut each pod from the fragile trees, using long poles to reach the higher fruits. The white seeds quickly change to a dark colour in the sun. They are heaped up in the sun and in a few days the flavours change from bitter to the cocoa taste we know. They are then spread out in the sun to dry completely.

## Bar

This is how you might see cocoa most of the time – in a bar of chocolate – where the cocoa has been mixed with other ingredients to make it solid and sweet. We sometimes melt the chocolate bar, or use chocolate chips to add to recipes. Cocoa is often used in sweet dishes, of course, but it is also used in many savoury dishes, like the popular Chilli con Carne. Other savoury dishes include sauces for barbecued meats, sticky pork ribs, and also in sauces called 'mole' from Mexico, which contain chilli, too.

# Peru

The potato, tomato and sweetcorn all come from here. Adventurous Spanish sailors, called Conquistadors, collected the seeds of these plants hundreds of years ago and took them home to Spain and Europe – so now we can all enjoy them.

This country is divided by the world's longest range of mountains, the Andes. They are home to the famous city of Machu Picchu, which was forgotten in the mountains for hundreds of years.

On the northern side of the mountains is the tangled Amazon rainforest.

The Peruvians are so proud of their cooking they never put salt and pepper on the table – they know it will taste just right!

in English: Beef kebabs

in Spanish: Anticuchos

Soaking the meat in oil and spices is called marinating. The flavours mix together to soak into the meat and also soften it.

# Beef Kebabs

Spicy kebabs like this are sold from street barbecues in Peru with a small baked potato on the end of the stick to make a quick hot meal that's easy to eat.

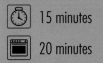

🕐 15 minutes

📟 20 minutes

🌡 Preheat to 180°C/350°F/Gas 4

Serves: 2 + 2

## To make:

1  **Cut the steak into pieces** about 2cm/¾in square, using scissors, and put in a bowl.

2  **Add the crushed garlic**, lime juice, chilli sauce, paprika, cumin, turmeric and pepper. Mix well, cover and leave for 30 minutes.

3  **Meanwhile, pop the peppers** (see Pop, page 13), then cut them into chunks, using scissors.

4  **Slide the beef carefully onto the soaked kebab sticks**, alternately with pieces of pepper. Don't put them too tightly together. Use all the meat and peppers – a little more for the adults.

5  **Line the baking sheet** with baking parchment (see Line, page 12). Brush the baking parchment with olive oil and lay the kebabs on top. Brush the kebabs with any leftover marinade and the oil.

6  🧤 **Ask your adult to put the baking sheet in the oven**, using oven gloves. Cook for 20 minutes or until the steak is brown and tender.

Serve with baked potatoes and roasted vegetables like peppers and courgettes/zucchini.

## Ingredients:

- 350g/12oz **beef steak**
- 1 teaspoon **ready-crushed wet garlic**
- 2 tablespoons **lime juice**
- 1 teaspoon **chilli sauce**
- 1 teaspoon **paprika**
- ½ teaspoon **ground cumin**
- ½ teaspoon **turmeric**
- 1 pinch of **ground black pepper**
- 2 **peppers** of any colour
- 2 tablespoons **olive oil**

## Extra equipment:

4 **bamboo kebab sticks** soaked in water, **pastry brush**

# Quinoa Salad

Quinoa is a tiny nutritious seed from the plant in the drawing that grows in the Andes mountains. You can buy it ready-cooked or dried, which you simmer in water or stock.

 20 minutes

Serves: 2 + 2

## Ingredients:

- 250g/9oz bag of ready-to-eat **quinoa**
- 1 tablespoon **corn oil**
- 1 tablespoon **lime juice**
- 1 **red pepper**
- 100g/3½oz **feta cheese**, cut into cubes
- 3 tablespoons canned **sweetcorn**
- 1 small easy-peel **orange**
- 1 **avocado**

## Extra equipment:

can opener

## To make:

1 **Put the quinoa into a serving bowl**. Sprinkle with the oil and lime juice and stir.

2 **Pop the pepper** (see Pop, page 13), then cut it into small pieces, using scissors, and put into the bowl. Add the cubed feta and the sweetcorn.

3 **Peel the orange** and cut each of the segments into 3, using scissors. This makes them easier to eat. Put the pieces of orange and any juice into the bowl. Stir well.

4 🧤 **Ask your adult to help you cut** around the middle of the avocado. You won't be able to cut it right through as there is a big stone/pit in the middle. Twist the two halves so they come apart, then take out the stone/pit. Scoop the flesh out of the skin with a spoon. Cut the flesh into 1cm/½in cubes, using a table knife, and add to the salad.

**Use the avocado skins as two bowls to serve your salad.**

We usually eat avocado as a savoury vegetable but it is really a fruit – actually a large berry!

in English: Quinoa salad

in Spanish: Ensalada de quinoa

in English: Chocolate cakes

in Spanish: Tortas de chocolate

Did you know that there is a World Chocolate Day? It is on 7 July and celebrated all over the world by people who love chocolate by baking and eating chocolate-flavoured things all day!

# Chocolate Cakes

There's a special extra sweet ingredient in these traditional mini chocolate cakes from Peru – the honey! The Peruvians have a very sweet tooth!

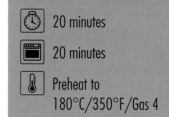

🕐 20 minutes

🍳 20 minutes

🌡 Preheat to 180°C/350°F/Gas 4

Makes: 8

## To make:

1 **Put the flour**, bicarbonate of soda/baking soda and cocoa/unsweetened chocolate powder into a mixing bowl. Stir in the sugar.

2 **Break the egg** into a cup (see Crack, page 11) and beat with a fork. Add to the bowl along with the milk and oil and mix well.

3 **Put the cupcakes papers in the holes** of the cupcake pan.

4 **Take a spoonful of the mixture** and use another spoon to push it into one of the cupcake papers (see Fill, page 12). Share out the mixture into the cupcake papers.

5 🧤 **Ask your adult to put the cupcake pan in the oven,** using oven gloves. Cook for 20 minutes until they have risen and spring back to a light touch.

6 **While they are still warm**, press a fork a few times in the tops to make holes. Drip the honey over the top, sharing it evenly among the cakes. Leave to cool.

7 **Once the cakes are completely cool**, spread the frosting over the top of each cake.

**These very sweet cakes are for special days – like birthdays!**

## Ingredients:

- 125g/4½oz/1 cup **plain/all-purpose flour**
- 1 teaspoon **bicarbonate of soda/baking soda**
- 3 tablespoons **cocoa/unsweetened chocolate powder**
- 45g/1¾oz/¼ cup **caster/superfine sugar**
- 6 tablespoons **milk**
- 2 tablespoons **corn oil**
- 2 tablespoons **clear honey**
- 8 tablespoon ready-made **chocolate frosting**

## Extra equipment:

12-hole **cupcake pan**, 8 **cupcake papers, cooling rack**

# Index

# NOURISH
## EAT WELL, LIVE WELL

Here at Nourish we're all about wellbeing through food and drink – irresistible dishes with a serious good-for-you factor. If you want to eat and drink delicious things that set you up for the day, suit any special diets, keep you healthy and make the most of the ingredients you have, we've got some great ideas to share with you. Come over to our blog for wholesome recipes and fresh inspiration – nourishbooks.com

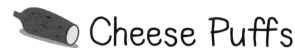 

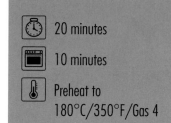

🌡️ Preheat to 180°C/350°F/Gas 4